SETTING THE POEM TO WORDS

for Cressy and Caleb

SETTING THE POEM TO WORDS

David Hart

- for Eleanor
with thanks
& best wishes
10.98
David.

Five Seasons Press
1998

Published in 1998
by Five Seasons Press
41 Green Street
Hereford HR1 2QH

Photoset in 11 on 14 pt Mergenthaler Sabon
at Five Seasons Press
and printed web offset
on Five Seasons recycled paper
by Biddles Ltd
Guildford and King's Lynn
(first use of 'Five Seasons recycled' for web printing)

British Library Cataloguing in Publication Data:
A catalogue record for this book
is available from the British Library

ISBN 0 947960 19 8

The publication of this book
would not have been possible without
the generous assistance of West Midlands Arts

Acknowledgements

'The silkies' won first prize in the Poetry Society's National Poetry Competition 1994. It was first published in *The Independent*, then broadcast on BBC Radio 4, published in the Poetry Society's *Poetry News* and in the Arts Council of England's Newsletter, then in the *Forward Anthology 1996*. 'Naming, my friends' won the Irish National Poetry Competition 1995 and was published in the *Birmingham Post* and in *Poetry Ireland Review*. 'Stretch marks' won joint first prize in the *Sheffield Thursday* magazine competition 1995 and was published in that magazine. 'With Nansen' was a prizewinner in the BBC *Wildlife Magazine* competition 1995. It was published in the magazine and broadcast on BBC Radio 4. 'Please bring some socks' won first prize in the 1995 *TOC H* competition and has been published in the *TOC H* magazine and recorded for an installation with the artist Sally Delany at Birmingham College of Art (UCE) 1996. 'This is the vessel' won first prize in the Lincolnshire Festival competition 1995 and has been published in *Oxford Poetry* and in the *Forward Anthology 1997*. 'Mr Lewis, Mr Howell, Mr Lloyd and myself' won a runner-up prize in the National Poetry Competition 1996, and has been published in *Writing in Education*. 'Love poem' won second prize in the Exeter competition 1997 and was published in the competition anthology. Other of the poems have won prizes in the following competitions: Surrey 1995, Ilkley 1995, Canterbury 1995, Bridport 1996, Age Concern (Stafford) 1997 and Lancaster 1997.

'Looking for God in the waters', 'Nine tables', 'Two other fellas' and an earlier version of 'A man called James Dye' were published in the limited edition *Forward: Labour & Art* (Birmingham City Libraries for National Poetry Day) 1997.

Other of these poems—some in earlier versions—have been published in *Poetry Wales*, *Poetry Review*, *Poetry Ireland Review*, *Sheffield Thursday*, *Raw Edge Magazine*, *Resurgence*, *Swansea Review*, *New Welsh Review*, *Shrike*, *Oasis*, *Obsession with Pipework*, *Heart Throb*, *Fire*, *Fatchance*, *Writing in Education*, *Prism International* (Canada), *The Interpreter's House*, *Sunk Island Review*, *Scratch*, *The Frogmore Papers*, *Rustic Rub*, *Tears in the Fence*, *Tandem*, *Illuminations* (USA), *Smiths Knoll*, *Fire*, *Leicester Print Workshop Artists' Book*, in the anthologies: *An idea of Bosnia* (Feed the Children 1996) and *Along the Line* and *Leaves at the World's Edge* (both Bishops Castle College, Shropshire), and read on BBC Radio 2.

When I have been asked about my poems I have heard myself saying that life itself is the strangest thing, being here, finding myself here, finding ourselves here. Publishing a book of poems on this planet spinning in space adds another strange aspect. I'm pleased to be doing it but in the whole scheme of things—what scheme?—there is, too, an absurdity about it.

We are all in this 'life' thing together, though, and I do want to take the opportunity to thank people who have in different ways shared and encouraged my making of poems, for whom whatever it is in us that makes poems necessary has mattered: Kim Taplin, Eleanor Cooke, Chris Meade, Sue Barlow, Dave Reeves, Stewart Brown, Gillie Bolton, Penny Smith, Bryan Podmore, Nigel Moffatt, Chris Carter and Richard Beaumond.

Thank you to Roy Fisher, Les Murray, Gillian Allnutt and Roger Garfitt, whom I have been fortunate to encounter in person and through their poems, for their quotable responses to mine. Thank you to West Midlands Arts for financial support. And not least I want to thank Glenn Storhaug for his Five Seasons generosity, patience and craft in the making of this book.

D.H. xii. 97

Contents

1

Naming, my friends

This is what we in this place call *seaweed*
and our name for this behind me is *sea*,
that over there we call an *island*,
this stuff we are standing on
has the name *sand*. In this way we build

our correspondences. For example, across the *sea*
you will find *seaweed* on the *sand*
at the *island*. We would go there if we had
the inclination in this *boat*. Feel the *boat*,

it is made of *wood*. Through the long Winter
sickness has made me its servant, and judging myself
to have been shifted aside from the everyday purposes
we hold in common for some other purpose
I have been rehearsing the names. This is *rock*, I believe,
which is a form of *sand*, this is *hand*
which is a form of *seaweed*,
this—move back a bit—is *spit*
which is a form of *sea*. Why have you come here

to visit me? You have nothing to say? Such grim smiles,
such nervous hands. This we call *rain*
which is a form of *sea*
which is a form of *spit*. This—hold up your hand—is *wind*

which is a form of *breath* you see squeezing through me
which is a form of *wave*. Have you been sent
by some agent or by inner intent
or did you arrive here merely wandering
as it might have been anywhere
by chance ? This we call *skull*
which is a form of *boat*. I shall not again be well.
This sound, my friends—look down my throat—is *talk*,

which is a form of *spit*,
which is a form of *rain*,
which is a form of *sea*.

Setting the poem to words

Then when we came into the empty market place
dragging our empty carts, empty in our stomachs
and in our hearts, almost stumbling every step

over the loose stones, feeling the sun burn as if
vengeful against us and us alone, a small flower
opened in the paving, coming up through dust,

and in one breath I wanted to put the poem
into words. But moving on was our everything:
water to be blessed if we could recall the tune,

prayers to be itched, fast dances to be trembled.
I heard or imagined I heard the story of a man
who tried to row, then carry, drag, then push

a crisp-clean boat across the clench of a desert,
cursing himself constantly for having started out.

The snail sets out up the steps

FOR KIM TAPLIN

In the sunshine the snail sets out up one step
where the steps are as firm as the sun itself,

each step closer to the core of the firm sun.
At every step a slate comes crashing away

from the snail's roof. Blind by the fifth step
the snail imagines the rest of the full hundred

and keeps going, each step hotter, the snail's
feet burn. Burnt through by the eleventh step

the snail heaves its stomach hot along and up,
imagining the full hundred. By the eighteenth

step all slates are gone and no skin remains
on its stomach, the snail balloons along on pouts

of air, burning along and up, listening now with
burnt-out ears for the nearer blessed silence

of the hundredth step.
When the snail's guts
are strung out between the nineteenth step

and the twenty-first still the ashen fibres
crave the hundredth and beyond the hundredth

and move on up.

The burning library

The artless smile of a child is a great portent,
it makes me think of a library burning.
The cockroaches and the spiders rush out
crushing the daisies with agility and speed.

The smile of the child whose little hand
is waving bye-bye, opening and shutting like a flower,
is a wonder. It makes me think of fruit growers
on an island drifting out to sea,
being taken far, far out into the ocean.

The wide open eyes of the child whose finger leaps up
pointing to a squirrel leaping from branch to branch
is beautiful. It makes me think of a gull
locked in a metal box, with no label. The box shines
with reflected light in a clearing
in the middle of an impenetrable forest.

So I must sit in the burning library and plan my work:
first to survey the library itself so as to feel at home,
next, to bring mist down around the fruit growers
until their island reaches the horizon
and falls over the edge.

After that, to locate the boxed gull, learn gullcraft
from the spirits of the falling leaves,
creep up on the gull in its metal box
according to instructions,
open the box wide
and ring its neck. I have been grown up a long time,

I have been of age as if it were already my old suit,
I have learned necessary guile and some tricks,
I have learned to sit patiently and write my plan,
I have learned expediency, I get things done.

So after all I am a playwright

So after all I am a playwright,
but a playwright of the empty stage.
Everything that happens happens in the wings
or in the wings of the wings
or around a corner or across the fields,

and although on good days, listening
I can hear a pin drop, a pin drop,
and I eat my sandwiches without crying,
the things that have to be written
who will speak them? Who will appear
with a sheet over their head, and their eyes closed,
and speak my lines?

Of course it's a celebration, every word,
being burned by the lights tells me that,
stage fright tells me that,
and the puppets in the cupboard tell me,
choosing this place
when they could live free in the forest.

Leaves at the world's edge

FOR BRYAN AND WENDY PODMORE

Leaves at the world's edge
for burial. No more to do

on the surface. *Let the new*
strike out towards the light,

says the poet, knowing it,
knowing too much of it. Mr Douglas,

collector of seeds
who fell into the pit full of wild bull

knew it. This is no pretty
migration of souls, no mouthful

to be processed for meaning
in the jaws of hell, no bridge,
no purge, there is no loving nudge,

this is the edge
beyond which words
only make
fools of themselves.

[David Douglas brought Douglas Fir seeds back from America, one of which seeded the tree at Walcot Hall, Shropshire—now the biggest of its kind in Britain.]

Holding the moment steady

I have the words *walk* and *alone* ready
but as soon as I apply these words
they do not speak for me properly.

Solitary and *trek* might be the words I need
or perhaps *anchorite* and *wander*,
but not one of these words is exactly right
and I am uncertain now what it is I do
or what condition I'm in really.

Without the right words
when *next week* or *next year* comes
I shall not be able to read what I had written and say,
ah yes, that was it, that was my life then.

I am in the conundrum of *walk, trek, solitary, alone,*
anchorite, wander. It is true that almost I can
sing these words
and they will approximate
but they are not precisely right.

Stride out and *unaccompanied*, these might do,
put one foot in front of the other, aloneness, with these
there could be sublime recognition, looking back.
But they won't do, they won't do at all.

Walk, rove—no, I don't *rove—shilly-shally,*
disappear up my own arse. The words themselves
don't know if they are right or not but they crowd me.
But I want the right words precisely
then I can speak for myself, can witness adequately
that I was here, on this *track* or *path* or *route*,
on this *way* or *pilgrimage*
or *frogmarch*. I am in *movement,*
I am conditioned. I have composed this *poem*
—or *song* or *text*—
and if it will *stay steady* or *remain steadfast*
or become *believable* or *reliable or* concupiscent,
if it will *speak*, then the *endeavour*
will appear to have been resolved.

2

Crag Inspector

HOLYHEAD MOUNTAIN, ANGLESEY

1.

Eight baby puffins impatient
to leap off the lower edges
and three still parents;

the black-eyed gull even sulkier
than usual, as if the best
fish of the night got away;

the dog daisy almost losing
its hold on the overhang
asks me nothing and I can do nothing.

2.
Doing my job
        by the letter
on good days
        by the spirit
I meet myself asking
awkward questions, the job a quarrel
between urgency
and patience.

I tell myself to speak
and to keep silent.

3.
There's a gull follows me around,
we are partial
to the same kind of biscuits.

Our planet is going into the darkness
of the dead. No-one will be here
to describe it as progress.

The pilgrimage daily
has to be kept in good nick
as the sun rises and sets,
all my surfaces.

4.
My irrelevant 'I', an itch
to the rock if the rock feels anything

ramparted by Celts
besieged by Romans
nailed by rock climbers
overflown by fighter jets
picknicked on by tourists
dynamited by quarriers
used for mere height by radar operators

the rock inspects me.

5.
All my foreshortened life
ever since I could run ahead
and get a grip on a crag
my eyes have been reflections of slate
flaking

from one day to the next,
from one week to the next,
from one month to the next,
from one year to the next. In the morning

I wake with their shapes in my mind
so that sometimes at breakfast
after an intense dream of flying
I am the mountain, its hardness,
its cracks and gullies. In the mist cormorants,
guillemots, gulls,
razorbills, puffins, occasionally
gannet, shearwaters and, I saw once,
an arctic skua,
have no statutory existence,
only presence.

6.
I do the job
day after day
and it makes a life.

Christmas comes
and Easter
and the tourist season,
I don't ask these times to come,
they come and I fit in,
and it makes a life.

7.
I return to my windowless hut,
a cliff cupboard really, no room
even for a chair. The whitewashed walls

are so white, so plain white,
glaring so white at me,
seeing what I see there
I think (and I like thinking)
I am going mad
while not knowing the difference.

I wonder sometimes if gulls
go mad, or crabs, or seals.
So far as I know I've never seen a mad one,

in fact the thought strikes me
as absurd. Back to work then,
keep a sandwich in my pocket
for later, my pencil needs sharpening,
I'll do that on the way up.

8.
I have seen silk scarves ooze out of crevices,
the tips of ladies' fingers come and go in the evening light,
I have seen a rupture open out of a pure green skirt
so that the spray wanted wiping from it with bladder wrack,
I have had ferns smoothing my way and holding me back,
shale has rolled me into the ocean almost.

9.
Off the mountain
I inspect cracks in pavements,
I inspect holes in bread,
I inspect fault lines in biscuits,
my home breaks slowly apart.

10.
Better to have your voice
taken away by the sea wind
than fill a large room
with every word heard.

11.
The dead razorbill
seems to have broken a leg
and torn a wing,
taken shelter
accepted death.

When I bury it under stones
other birds collect themselves overhead,
hover as if through a window,
now let themselves be taken by the wind.

12.
I am unable to speak,
I hesitate,
I begin sentences—people wait,
more often a tree, an outcrop,
a gull—I begin sentences
and I don't complete whatever it was.

Something speaks.
The people who constructed with stone and turf
circular houses on the slopes
of the mountain,
they speak to me still.

Something speaks.

The Romans who conquered in Latin, long
marching columns of it along long straight roads

of it to build high slate walls of it,
they speak to me still.

Something speaks.

Something else, something else,
something I can't explain,
something that comes with the job.
Have I spoken about the terrors?

The visits.

As if I were not born.

Or knew too much.

As if I shall be wandering down there
          on the lowest grass above the sea
and be found by chance by my closest
who will not recognize me

but will instead days later
report me missing.

13.
I might tell you about the writing I have seen
running along the sheer faces after rain
from crag to crag, or when I've been tired at the end
of a hot day, but honestly I can't say

I've ever been able to decipher it. The signs,
you understand, the inherent speech of the rock,
its necessary speech. I could ask myself again
say Friday week and see if I have better luck.

3

The child following me

The child wants to come with me
but I say let him find his own way
and I go on without him.
He catches up with me crying
quietly to himself, saying his own way
is no way at all. Across the meadow
I can hear the daisies growing
and I say again
everyone must find their own way
but the gulls disagree with me,
wanting the child at least allowed
to tag along, using my direction,
so I relent and he follows on
cautiously, staying several yards behind me
when I stop to eat, sleeping
in a separate hedge, killing
his own rabbit. And to himself
he talks continually night and day,
arguing, I suppose, his good case.

Harbour boy

I was a harbour boy.
I watched when the lifeboat was launched
and when the band played and when couples kissed
on the end of the jetty in the warm wind.
I watched as fish in boxes slithered
and tried to jump at their wits'
and their lives' end. I lived from feeling to feeling,
not from day to day.

I thought some fish had human eyes.
The old woman who sat apart
with her eyes set tight
staring into the waves
surely had lived under the sea. I would watch a gull
glide up and up until pure gliding
seemed to replace the need for mackerel. My own gut
was the serpent shape shown by the patterns
met by sunlight on the sea as it swirled in and out
between the jetties. I was unable

either to be circumspect
or to be bold. The wind knew, as it passed,
all my secrets, even the secrets so secret
they were promises only
and still hidden from me. My soul is burned

with salt, there was a battleship once,
anchored in the bay, I suppose indicating victory.
The trip boat out swayed at the foot of its steps,
the ship was grey and smelt frugal, dank, unnaturally tight,
it might have come from another planet
where there is no childhood, then one day
it went away, leaving me on the wall
and the porpoises far out
to our own speculations. Let me be clothed

in seaweed, let the popping of the seeds
be my music, let me wear those shiny scarves,
that slippery skirt with light dissolved in it,
let me hear the turning of the stones
in the rocking cot, let my heart ache,
let me know always
the clean wrench of the tides.

I can act brilliant mad

FOR MY SON CALEB

I can act brilliant mad,
like I can fall off the chair
into the painted river on the floor,
I can swim for my life,
I can be a poisoned bear desperate for water
and at the same time I can sing hymns
silently at the top of my voice. I can cry
at the beauty of the hills at dawn, I can
act weightless and fall off the world
into endless space, I can build a cottage
out of toilet roll holders and spend my holiday in it,
I can teach a hedgehog the Highway Code,
I can remember everyone's loved ones killed in accidents
by flying paper aeroplanes with their names on
from a motorway bridge. I can play marbles
with a sparrow's eggs. Easy.

With Nansen

When I was ten I went in search of the north pole with Nansen.
From the New Siberian Islands where we'd left the Fram locked
in ice we walked into white light. Nourished by broken biscuits

and Wagon Wheels and spied on by nosy seals and furtive foxes
we hacked through homework with picks and looked forward
to football on Saturday, hoping for floods of sunshine to dry out

the boggy field. On the first Sunday in the month we paraded
the colours into church and sang plaintive and patriotic hymns,
and when first we tried to kill a whale hurling our spears after

several days in wait we finished up feeling stupid and cold,
exhausted and longing for some steamed chocolate pudding
and seconds in the playground through the kitchen window,

then a bear protecting her cubs growled at us,
then we tried to send a telepathic message
back to Mr Thomas to say we were doing our best,
then we played marbles in the tracks of lemmings,
then we lit a fire and baked potatoes in its embers,
then we bet each other toffees we couldn't turn
somersaults on a moving ice-flow,
then we buried a grass snake under snow and moss
and over its poor head placed a twig cross,
then I dreamed I met the abominable snowman
and was pleased to wake to the sound of gulls,
then I made snow-castles with my bucket and spade,
then Nansen received a telegram from the King
brought by a strong and courageous pigeon,
then we reached 86° 14′ and after the flag was planted
we wintered there in Franz Josef Land,

and when me and Nansen got home again from our expedition,
in front of the whole school assembly we received our book token,
and after shaking hands warmly we went our separate ways.

The treasure

I am tremendous lonely, Sir,
and I can't find the treasure.
I think I've seen the signs, Sir,
but where they point nothing's there.

I can't hear you, child,
I'm lost here and old,
deaf now and cold.
in this twilight field.

I can't find the treasure, Sir,
and soon it will be night.
I'm tremendous lonely, Sir,
and soon we will have no light.

I can't hear you, child,
I'm lost here and old,
deaf now and cold
in this twilight field.

Promenade with carnival

Pulling back the curtain on a wet June afternoon
I see the carnival: girls in tinsel,
a solemn boy in armour killing for ever
a papier-mâché dragon, then the tin-whistle band
leading the royal float of the lovely Queen Of The Fishes
dripping with smiles. And running alongside her waving
a child

stumbles and falls. Always someone has to be
the baby of the whole family, starting again, at first
imprecisely, not yet comprehending like God
the entire world. The child gets up, runs a little more,
but now is sitting squat on the pavement,
her head in her hands. Here in my house everything
is in its right place: the pings of spoons,
shells with the shifts of the sea in them,
remembered hurts, a cormorant chick in a bottle,
flaking lead soldiers,
fragments of songs as I move from room to room,
pictures of ruined arches.

A wave comes over the sea wall like sperm
spraying the majorettes. The task is to tell the truth
but what truth? The child is up again
running and shouting, she is older,
it is almost Winter.

If the soul of my dead father

ABERYSTWYTH, SEPTEMBER 1997, I.M. ALFRED HART D. 1962

If the soul of my dead father remembers anything
he will remember the rake of these rock pools, the lean
of their stacked lines, he will note limpets and shrimps
and know this umbrella mist as it falls lightly as drizzle.

If he remembers anything he will hear the clipped whisper
of the waves on the turn, here where he used to swim
far out as if—I wonder now—it was his only solitude.
I suppose a soul from this place will hear gulls squeaking

and have no argument with far-sighted oblique storms.
'High tides are expected', a woman said to me today,
my father's soul will want to be here, in the spray
and in the gale, in the storm's uncompromising rage.

Hanging loose

I find myself hanging loose around you
in the kitchen, hanging like washing too
damp for folding back into the cupboard

as if about to ask an awkward and urgent
favour or say shyly slouching I've bent
the rules or worse and must confess charred

remains of a fire in me, or that I have
decidedly burned my bones and must give
notice. I could say in truth radiant sunshine

makes me cry, or, *There are perhaps*
good reasons for thinking, dear,
everything's all right. But no, each day

here on the linoleum a distant song
never gets sung, no rose pops up
magically out of my buttonhole,

the cat swaggers in, demands her tea,
then settles herself down
in a warm place, whole and comfortable.

I like it here, it's lovely, beautiful, beautiful

CARDIGANSHIRE, AUGUST 1996, FOR CRESSY AND CALEB

Bog. Three sheep. Narrow stony track. Rushes.
Field open to the erratic gods of all the winds.
Dark clouds coming from the West over ridges
of chewed tough grass, rocks showing through.
To the south a valley side with some cultivation,
a variety of greens and browns, hedges of trees.
To the north, bushy white clouds travelling faster.
Fence on the horizon. On the near slopes
pine trees, great geometric blocks of them
with pocky patches grey after felling and clearing.
A sheep near me baas, jumping through heather.
Facing east again, the warmth on my back is exquisite;
there are flicks of cold breeze, then bigger scuffs of it,
then pure warmth again, all of a piece, everything right
as it is and for this short time us, too, right in it.

4

You know the story

You know the story of the man who
in the impulsive moment in prayer
alone in the ancient chapel rises
from his knees and thieves
the sandstone carving of the saint
with his fingers raised in blessing,
prising it away easily but sweating
from its makeshift modern putty
in the niche in the sanctuary wall
and takes it home under his coat
and with his heart thumping hides
it away in the wardrobe wrapped
in the warm blanket behind the shirts
and the socks, behind the neckties
and the trousers and the jackets
and the Christmas decorations,
behind the cricket whites, you know
this story, how it continues and ends.
Terrible, terrible, terrible, terrible.

Morning raga

On the third day as soon as the moon allows
the woman runs towards the glowing tomb

without sleep, crossing the river, kicking stones
in her haste, disturbing sheep, losing a sandal,

rushing through the traders setting up their stalls,
thanking the light, riding the planet,

testing phrases, opening up her lungs,
steadying her hands to touch, trusting the dust.

The big name

AT PENNANT MELANGELL

In the little house
of the big name
(in the valley
with the buzzards
and the sheep),

at the altar of
the little house
of the big name
(in the clearing
with the graves
of the poor who stayed),

in the regular singing
at the altar
of the little house
of the big name
(where the yew trees
predate the big name's son

when he was on our planet
speaking
in the big name's name),
I can't forget
my own
but clothe it
with stone.

No sooner have I eaten

No sooner have I eaten
than the food is pecked out of me.

I eat again,
it is pecked out of me again.

You see this hole in my chest ?
You see this blood-grill chest ?

Those gulls on the sea wind
have never had enough,

they turn and turn again
and I shall eat to death.

The man whose job it is

The man whose job it is to replace the binoculars in their sockets
at the opera house, those left under the seats, in the bars, in the toilets,
sits on the beach watching the tide go far, far out with gulls on it.

He drags his sleepy limbs up on all fours, and growls at the sea,
making it go even further away. He bounces, he does a circling jump,
he rolls into a ball, he lies back flat, and stares deep

into the sky. The stage with no end catches him unaware,
it's the sore, raw, ineloquent, blunt off-guardedness we're for.

We led the trembling

We led the trembling, hesitating animals
across the ledge of rock between the dunes.
Our muttered oaths invoked the God who reigns
but no-one looked for corporeal sentinels
more eloquent than sand or wind or sun,
for we were lost and could blame no-one.

The little man

The body behind the grill in the shrine has its skin undone
and out pops a little man singing bright hymns to the moon,
and as passers-by pass by in whispered conversation
and are asked by the little man the way to Moon Mountain,
they remember as if long, long ago an enchanted englyn,
and as they day-dream the man waiting to know is drawn
back under the body's skin, never again to be heard or seen.

The blackbirds

FOR GLENN STORHAUG

In the morning we could hear no blackbirds singing in the woods,
so we shot them out of the tall trees and ordered them to sing.

When they refused to sing we cooked them for breakfast,
when they sang in our stomachs we danced in their honour.

Wings

The butterfly's wings are becoming so heavy they touch
the ground almost, they hit the hawthorn and get thrown
sideways by the spray from the waterfall miles away.

They no longer fold into land only fall splayed. The perceiving
of what was familiar needs impossible translation. Every field
rolling green has its beautiful crashed aeroplane.

O strange animals

O strange animals
that care in us,

strange strong animals
lie waiting for an end in us,

oh dry animals
that mourn in us,

coiled serpents
are knotted in us,

rare butterflies
look for flowers in us,

dear dark animals
stretch dying in us,

bats fly in circles
in our caves,

oh strange animals
heal us.

Pure white iguana

A pure white iguana has entered the pure white room
and the name of the iguana is *iguana, purest white*.
And the pure white walls catch their breath, the pure
white door opens and closes, the pure white wind
that breezed in for a moment lingers and sways.

For I am in the iguana, I am its pure iguana nature,
when I hear the name *iguana, purest white*, I merge
myself with the pure white room and am at home.

Outside the pure white room in the pure dark, steamy
blessed corridor my friend the pearly gleckny fish
swims up and down in anticipation of my success
but nervously. I have no prior or serene knowledge.
I am here alone *iguana, purest white* in the room

that I begin to recognize is my own. Shall I be pure
here for ever? Shall my simple pure whiteness merge
with the pure white room's for ever? Be calm, lover,

be as calm as cloud, as calm and undecided as calm
storm cloud. Take off the mask of purest white, speak
and be born storm. Lost lover, be born as storm,
pretend to storm, try storm on, wear storm, shape
when the bell rings in the pure white heart yourself

into undecided storm. Gleckny fish swims gloomily
up and down believing all is lost. Oh my friend fish,
oh my true-born storm, gluttonous, lusting friend fish.

The garden

'They wandered in the still air with a stark quality like that of nudity.'

THOMAS HARDY, TESS OF THE D'URBEVILLES

Now that everything has burned down
I must ask the pigeon
and the feral cat
and the cabbage white
what wisdom is

to start again. Behind the scorched hedge
the hand rots that wound the clock,
that pruned the cherry
and held me. I can hear a bucket falling
and pouring out its water

but it comes too late
from the heavenly place
that had sucked it up. A window is here alone

hanging in the air. I can look through it
and over it and under it
and beyond each side of it. My eyes
burned out of their holes

are everywhere. Let us walk then, you and I
nakedly.

The great sad General

FOR GUL DAVIS

He does not pass by but crouches low as low,
he buries his face in the earth, this earth we know,

faint music—listen—floats by us slowly
—it is the great sad General singing shyly.

A god who is asleep in parts of his territory
is here with the great General singing shyly.

Close to death the great General sings shyly
here where the battle is a cracking memory.

An athlete with his head in a towel brightly
promenades across the great plain of despondency

while the great General continues to sing shyly
as if at one with the wounded earth's reverie.

The ship is coming

The ship will get through,
the ship will get through,
but it will not get through,
there is no god to bring it.

The ship will get through
without any god's breath,
the ship will plough through
with its great engines.

The ship's crop will fail,
there will no harvest,
there is no urgency at all,
the ship will not come through.

The ship will cut through,
it will sew itself through the sea,
it will wear our clothes
with our hearts in them.

The ship will not get through,
the ship's engines will stall,
the ship's hold will storm-flood,
the ship will not get through.

The ship will appear at last,
we will see the ship at last,
but the ship will be in splinters,
we will see only sinking splinters.

The wood will hold together,
we will see the wood shine,
we will see the shining wood
coming wholly through to us.

Does it matter, really,
whether the ship comes or not?
It does matter.
it does matter.

Room

IN THE MARK ROTHKO ROOM AT THE TATE GALLERY

Who enters here does not enter.
Who prays here aloud stays silent.

The walls echo back no presence.
Light-of-Light storms illuminate nowhere.

I need somewhere to stay, I can't wander for ever,
if I can find a home I can be a person.

A file on the elegant shovelling in and out of personality
is opened and closed, opened and closed.

I can't feel what I can't feel in this no-space,
the walls smell of a far away land in which to wander.

The strong ship arrives but with no cargo, no hold,
no frame, no length, no weight.

If I can find a home I can be a person.
Time carries me on whether I like it or not.

The blast of the trumpet pursuing me
was never a sound only a hole in the sky.

The dumb, lonely scream of the heart
claims and disowns sight.

Time carries me on whether I like it or not,
home clutches my heart, I need somewhere to stray.

This I-assuming fragment asks, Will there be grainy,
felicitous, radiant, richly paradoxical music ?

Home clutches my heart, I need somewhere to stray,
I can't stray for ever, I need somewhere to rest.

Seraphic thugs from inner space
demand protection money: flesh, flesh, flesh.

The teacher's heart is cold in its box.
I need somewhere to stay, I can't wander for ever.

The I-assuming fragment fumbles to explain its terrible
invisible bright longing and the thugs spit.

[CONTINUED

I can't rest for ever, I need somewhere to wander,
straying and resting blur, bleed, bleed, blur.

This district the world, roofless hall of memory
spills the red of bleed, the grey of blur, the blue of drift.

Time continues to float the me I happen to be.
I don't know what I don't know in this no-mind.

This fiercely floodlit shed with the vaulting blown off
spills the red of bleed, the grey of blur, the blue of drift.

The angel of homecoming hovers, hovers and waits.
I need somewhere to wander, I can't rest for ever.

5

All this time

All this time I've been in my hut on the edge of the desert
hanging out my washing, harvesting the milkweed,
feeding the bony goat, and I hadn't noticed the little man

away by the rocks tending his fire or sitting in prayer
or as if shaping the air. Has he ever seen me sweating here ?
I would have hid from his intense eyes.

Are my rehearsed dance steps a sham ? My voice, is it a mere
mechanical squeak, stolen from a bottle of pop opening?
The little man with the chirpy help of small birds is arranging

his piles of twigs. A kangaroo I've never known was here
brings the little man water, tipping it out of its large pouch
into a stone bowl. I shrink back and watch through a crack

between the boards of my hut. I rest my hand on my table
and dust flies up all around my face, blinding me. I so want
to be ancient and done with it, to have been and gone.

The little man laughs and this brightness echoes around
the whole universe except in my hut. A swaggering fox
comes over the ridge and licks the little man's feet fresh.

All the good lies I've told. Look here are some of them
inscribed on the walls of my hut. My secret. But if you arrive
when I'm out you will find the place guarded by a python,

I call it in from the scrub when I need a special favour.
I feed it ideas, suggestions, survival techniques, wriggles
and twists, grips, turns and strikes new and delightful to it.

The little man has seen me and is slowly approaching.
As he comes closer he is becoming smaller, thinner, wispier
and now almost about to arrive at my door he is nothing.

I must feed the goat some olive leaves it is unable to reach
and milk the weed to keep myself in some sense alive.
And bring my washing in and arrange myself for sleep.

This is the vessel

This is the vessel. The bodies, as you can see,
have rotted further since I sent you the note,

and couch grass has begun to grow through the deck.
Where there was a log book there is now pulp.

I have done my best with devotion hoping you'd come;
I was a bright lad at school, though inward and shy.

Before you make your inspection of the remains
inch by inch perhaps you would like lunch: aperitif

squeezed fresh from wild raspberries, then nettle soup,
main course of Rock Salmon, a slippery

Orange Squash I've been keeping cool in the river,
goosegog dumplings to follow, then a tea bag

preserved these years in dock leaves. I crave
company but without your permission

I shall inflict on you no conversation,
and after a short sleep you can soldier on

through what's left of daylight into the night.
It is entirely up to you, I am your servant.

The body in the bluebells

I found a body in the bluebells snuggled in,
laid down by the stream, bent, playing dead.
Anyone is allowed to play dead, their ration
of dead, to discover the world. Ferns flattened

and bramble even flattened and of course
bluebells as exquisite as any I'd seen walking
in the woods there year after year. An angel
that serves warm bread at the border waiting

seemed to be present, not stone with a trumpet
nor the embroidered sort nor gilded wax
nor painted, none of those, but humanly patient
and blue, undecided, slight and wanting sex.

So here was an angel randy around the body,
longing to be earthy. We were at the margin,
almost I had a foot in it. Should I tell the story?
Should I tell of the bright angel's longing?

I ate my sandwiches and my cake and drank
water from the stream, with blood in it, reader.
Someone would in turn find me, blue, sunk
in the job of being found, of being found there.

The hesitation waltz at twilight in Jane's field

Between Broad Meadow and the North Field
with Dark Lane running along the bottom,
Jane's field was turned over that special night
to the having-a-good-time for everyone project.

Jane had showed me long since her slant field,
started to show me, was called away, by bleating,
and I'd sat then, suspended in space and time,
with my head in my hands as if the upper

of the three worlds was about to compress me,
us, and I was fearful, breathing my very last,
I thought, in utter panic, while dear, still Jane
helped the ewe, easing out together a lamb.

I've walked the field many times alone, around it,
through it from gate to gate, along Dark Lane
and beyond that, set in its gulley, the river
with its own path, muddy often, worn away.

Oh there were fifty, more, people that night,
excited hot and cold as the sun went down,
one joker rolled over and over into the hedge,
I wanted to do it but was stuck fast. A waltz now,

Jane announced, and we two winced and glowed
and found each other, we knew who we wanted,
shyly we knew, and there was a band, perched
like all of us on the slope, it was crazy, lovely.

And so we danced the formal hesitation waltz,
both of us hesitant and both raring to go.
We seemed to have many more legs than four
yet somehow we didn't trip or bruise or lose

hold of each other. And the next day I cried
all along Dark Lane, slipping down to the path
along the river, up into Broad Meadow,
through the beech wood, sobbing my heart out.

The silkies

Someone last Autumn put the evil eye on Mrs Kendrick
for hanging bright crimson knickers on the line
in sight of where the boats come in,

and as the word got around the island
still the knickers flew there,
and they flew through last week's luminous storms
and through the lovely day we had on Sunday
when Jock proposed to me. Nobody of us

has spoken to Mrs Kendrick all these winter days. My dream
last night told me everyone has been cleared out
and that in the stolen land Mrs Kendrick alone remains,
she is hiding in a cave
below the water line
diving and gliding and eating blenny and shanny with the seals
and whispering to them at the hurt reach of her voice,
It's all you've got
wear the sea close, then she bleeds
all the way home; she is wearing a room
where the plaster flaps off the walls
revealing pictures of the hosts of hell,
dead pelicans queue on the roof,
cupboards sag full of uneaten meals,
windows have layers of faces fingered into their dew,
yet the wreath of roses on the door
drips loveliness. Boats fill the harbour,

it's the time of year, Mrs Kendrick makes red hot jam
for any captain away from home that wants it
on his night toast, I kiss Jock

on his rough lips in the shadows.

Betty asks, *Who owns the world?*

Betty, packing her things to go, asks, *Who owns the world?*
I want to say gladly, *We all do*, but it sticks in my throat.
Anne says, *God does*, and there is an exhausting silence.

Whenever Cherry comes out of silence she looks glazed.
Betty asks, *Are you still with us, dear?* and Jane answers,
Is she, hell?! She's away with the fairies. We all
cock our heads to listen in on Cherry's other world,
except Betty who swings her bag and starts to leave.
Jane waves her away, *See you in the morning*, she says, *early*.
Betty, confused, ambles out, in no hurry.
Jane wants to feel Cherry's pulse but Lorraine, getting in first,
gives Cherry some menu paper and a felt-tip pen.

Betty pops her head back in, asking again, *Who owns
the bloody world?* meaning it. Lorraine, turning to me,
spells it out, mouthing the words, *Not the likes of us*,
and adds, aloud, *dear!* Cherry writes: 'Keeping low
over the river's long body
I am a young dragonfly, the sun is on my back,
it is too much for me to carry. If I can't fly
the river will swallow me.' Then she says, *Christ, I'm thirsty!*,
and Betty, dropping her bag, rushes to switch the urn on.

Over tea, our mugs half way to our lips,
after we've passed round what Cherry has written—
as if there's more to it in the very handwriting
and looking for tear stains and even blood—
Jane sighs, and looks at Cherry and says, *Is that it?!*
This lacks courtesy and I want to say, *We all own it,
the world, I mean*. But Anne's face is still washed hurt
in her ineffable God. Betty melts slowly away.
Cherry's bright eyes let out big, chrysalis tears.

Is this really how it always has to be, our separateness
the very consequence of ecstasy ? Jane shrugs her shoulders,
despairing of us. Anne bites her lip. Lorraine's eyes blaze.
Betty is back muttering, *I've left my keys*. I want to say,
No one does, no one owns the world, or *We all do,*
but I'm bent over and shaky and I turn away.

Love poem

This is my daft husband, godforsaken, lost.
His name is writ in syrup and at best
he can name an oak and sing when he's pissed.

He wasn't a country lad, the great city
spewed him out. I was young and took pity,
I thought I was marrying a man whose tightly

packed grin held secrets more venturesome
than Elvis and he could make me come
like no boys in the village had. He called me scum

first on our honeymoon, then did a handstand
—we were on a foreign beach, Ibiza, Cyprus, Ostend,
I don't remember which—then turned me round

and we danced and drank all night. I was sick
but happy. He was weird, I'd turned my back
on boredom—at school I'd watched the clock.

'Everyone knows the score,' he said one wet day
years later, and I had nothing to say, bled dry,
crying inside, then said he craved my body.

We play poker some nights and I let him win.
He tells me the same jokes again and again.
He says he's not religious but it would be a sin

to leave him. I smile a bit and fetch another beer,
God and the angels have forsaken him, I'm sure,
but he's my daft husband and he's living here.

Our holiday on research money

He said he was researching care so we went on holiday
with his grant money. It rained and mostly we played
pool with mates he found the first night and I learned

to play not at all badly. But wandering away by myself
was the best part, finding the path over the crinkly cliff top,
picking the last blackberries, watching for silver dolphins

I believed might just be there. He shouted in my face,
said I'd deserted him, said I made him look stupid in front
of the other blokes, said he'd paid. I went out again next

morning, along an old track, the sun was pouring into it
between the trees. I said to myself I was being photographed
by angels, and later I was about to tell him this, pretending

to forget his shouting of the day before, when he hit me.
In the room, in the *en suite* room, very private, very special
to us, he'd said, and I'd laid my silk scarf out like a cloth

over the little table, to prepare as it were a sacrament
of our being there. I suggested we could walk together,
but he said if he'd wanted to walk he'd have hired a dog.

It didn't hurt, not the shouting, not the slap round the face,
not the sarcasm, and I puzzled over this when I was walking
the next morning again, when I was walking very quietly

across a boggy meadow, everywhere misty, some blue light
coming through, the angels doing their best, maintaining
I told myself, a presence, holding me, keeping in touch.

My night bag was an encumbrance, a suitcase not being made
for hill-walking, but it had a packet of custard creams in it now
and a bottle of wine, for the summit, before the train home.

His wife drove him always

His wife drove him always,
the Impressionists had washed him out,
had done for him altogether.

He sometimes liked a cream tea
if the drive was not too arduous,
and she found it for him.

The Impressionists had done his head in.
As he was driven the memories came,
a clotted scream—she would joke with friends

after he'd died, after she'd last driven him,
giving them always more impressions,
laying his life out for them—escaped him.

She drove him to the end, always,
no conversation clouded the journeys,
she had learned to enjoy silence.

He feared for his soul's peace beyond death,
the thought of eternal Impressionism
terrified him. She laid her hand

on his arm. She placed a leaf
in his open hand, and she spoke its name: *leaf, leaf.*
He woke as if from an amputation.

His wife drove him always,
they were in relationship,
a miracle was not expected.

She drove him quickly through mountains,
when a gull flew overhead near the sea
she said nothing, nor at sunset.

His wife drove him always,
she was his ears and eyes,
the Impressionists had washed him clean out.

The scrubbing of the walls

A someone was sudden and solid here by us
for three days
scrubbing our walls. We sat silented, we worked our eyes
hard out, we shivered, we were too frighted
to ask an eventual
or sigh deep sick or spurt up giggles with joy

because she was beautiful. These were my
rubbing against walls, and my life's nails
has scratch them and my life's mouth
has talk into them. I knew from touch them or fixed
runny eye every creep of their rough,
but now in this light when *I know* comes out
or *I knew* or *I did know, I did, I did,* shame

squirms around in the landscape in me, this me,
the me I was before
inside the me I am today *know*. Then she wasn't here.
I try to split open these words at my life: *I know these walls,*
I knew them, I did,
tiny whispery, and now, *tiny whispery,* then, *God in his love,*
and eyeing us, too,
the us I know or knew, I did know, I did,
the us as old rough walls knowing us stood by.
She was beautiful but this wall
doesn't smell now of us, it smells scrubbed of know,
it smells of her work three days. Scrub fingers out, out, out
for *know*, the walls
beg the little me in me for *know*, they want dream but I dare not
drag my whole *I am* up from my corner,
I dare not suggest to the *me in the room*, I dare not do any make.
I say, *suggest*, I mean *want, I want*,
I mean, *cry out, I cry out,* I mean *I want to cry out: These walls*

must show my films! Spiders were here
and cockroaches.

Sheela's poem, sectioned again

I entered the enemy's house, being as hungry
as a bee in a world of dead flowers.
In the enemy's house flowers
were in full bloom and I needed them,
I needed their fragrance and their nectar to fill me.

Where is my friend now who was clever,
who stayed outside with her hunger?
She gave me a buzz,
our voices gave us poems in the shadows of days,
how is she now in her hunger?

They have named me cripple again,
they have fed me dullness.
They have taken away my own true name,
the name *friend*, they will feed me,
trying to inhabit my whole body
with dullness, dullness, dullness
until I'm a beautiful, gutted ruin.

I need to fly, I need to be able and aware
in my own body to fly.
There is plenty of air out there to fly in.
Voices, tell me how to fly,
fly me to my friend,
fly me out again to share the great hunger.

Will my friend write the hunger poem now?
Will she write the terrible hunger?
There is an assembly of hunger,
it meets at the Centre,
they are piss-heads and angels,
she can read her rich poem there.

Alone with our brains

Some iron pipes have been left in Angie's brain.
She told me so herself
last Friday, when we walked together in the mist,
stepping over dead sheep.

There's a log hut in my brain, I said, with a door
and one small window;
it's draughty, I said, but okay when the sun shines.
Angie was happy at that,
pleased for me. She said sometimes there's gurgling
in the iron pipes in her head
and sometimes a grating and scuffling noise
as if someone desperate
is trying to clamber through. The mist lifted now
and the dead sheep
came back to life, grinning as resurrected sheep do,
and we did a little dance.

I told Angie she could stay in the hut in my brain
if she was in town
and needed somewhere to stay. She said she'd love to
but the iron pipes, she said,
wouldn't fit into my hut, and we spent the afternoon
on the dewy slopes
trying to work out how to overcome this problem.
We concluded it was hopeless
but that we'd enjoyed the attempt. A gun came at us
as if from nowhere then
and demanded our lives unless a ransom was paid,
and we explained.

We explained that with the iron bars in Angie's brain
and the hut in mine
no-one would dream of paying out a large even a small
sum to get us returned safely.

We felt sorry for the gun as it wobbled away
dolefully into a gully,
but we were gladdened, joyful even, to have discovered
how truly lost we were, how alone.

The journey

I wear around my neck the bags of my necessities—
the grasses, ash, a dead leaf, a tuft of goat's wool
and red tincture, together with seeds from the skies.

I am ready now to face the journey so forgive me
if my voice fades out suddenly. I have some guile
but not sufficient yet and may pay the penalty.

If angels come skimming after me laugh them away,
they will enjoy laughter and not take offence.
They mean well but don't know the tracks or sway

of the body's bounce into the particular sharp wind.
If a man comes panting, hurt, make allowance,
for he will be my unincorporated self, he will find

if he persists something resembling what he knows
but all my life he has been behind, out of breath,
or ahead and sleeping, or alongside me, his eyes

everywhere until what was possible is again lost.
If an animal comes making songs full of wrath
respect it, give the creature space, let the dry past

and the premeditated future hear it. If any of you
think to follow me, let it be provisional. As invisible
as you will appear, you must put on a good show

or I am lost. Promote your invisibility with flowers
and drums and all the perfumes of the ignoble.
Bring rain, dance the sun, be the moon's whores.

In the market

FOR SUE BARLOW

No-one comes checking names, aliases, faces
against an old, torn passport, disbelieving,
but she passes the stalls—asparagus, hot bread—
as if at any moment she will be confronted.

Stooped and shaky she creeps between the stalls
by invisible stepping stones from smoked ribs
to beetroot to brass pots to shoes to cottons
past stacks of old books to the coins and candles.

Slipping in as the traders clearing their stalls
of leftover plums, onions, mutton and scrag-end
of books joke about the day's wearying business
she sings silently calling the storm to take her.

Now her skipping between the stalls is a fling.
Looking to the widest sky she can find
she welcomes the clouds, their exaggeration,
their lushness. She seems to know now

what she came here running for, who she is.
Every splash on every vegetable and fruit
is a kiss, she opens herself to the kisses
and would have the rain make love to her wholly.

Someone throws a book. It flies like an octopus
over stalls and heads, and lands at the woman's feet
after splashing her hair and her shoulder.
She steps aside from it as from a fetid carcass.

Now she has fallen back heavy into the shadows
stroking a cat, feeling her way along a wall
until, curving around, the cold of it reaches the river
where she splashes her hands freely in the water.

Now she is running her tired restless fingers
along the washed wood of the empty stalls.
The scent of the juice of apples floats bitter-sweet
on the darkness. An alert rat stops, sits up, listens.

So we did as we were told

So we did as we were told and stood in line facing forward,
hands at our sides, feet together, cold with no clothes on.

I'd stood like this in front of T. for a moment late at night
but that was different, willed, a risk, of course, but meant.

Were we and them the last people left in the whole world?
The tellers and the told together for one last confrontation?

R., beside me, tried not to shiver and I wanted to link arms,
but P. and J. who did this furtively are no longer with us.

Will I remember these words which I keep repeating over,
which I repeat and improve if I can a little, then add a stanza,

without moving my lips? Y.'s lips moved, she is no longer
with us. A picture forms in my mind of K., my brother,

throwing me into mown grass, a whole heap of it, laughing,
and I laughed, too. He was soon swimming, spluttering,

back out of the river. I want to grin now but my face
must be frozen. L. smiled at dawn and is no longer with us.

A shiver has travelled the whole of E.'s body, involuntarily,
E. is no longer with us, only the remnant now of E.'s family.

I hadn't thought we would end like this. Two weeks ago
I borrowed jam from S. when we had guests, E. and O..

I'd baked an apple cake, had brought the elderflower wine
to perfection, we sat in the kitchen giggling, O.'s eyes shone.

What will this matter, that it must be passed on in a poem,
what will it matter knowing we did this or that in a room?

We are aware of each other's nakedness, precious, lovely
and expendable. I can see only out of the edge of my eye.

C.'s eyes turned to look along the line, in some distress.
V.'s eyes responded, N.'s too, and are no longer with us.

The sunlight falls smack

The sunlight falls smack against the whole of the wall.
It is as if only this one side of the building exists.
It is as if this smooth, windowless wall is itself
the source of light. But around the other side
of the echoing building people are in tears.
Their bags and their bodies
are being taken away from them. How to go on
without a body? The light shifts

imperceptibly but enough for a margin
down the east end to darken. It makes me shiver
but from the ninety-nine per cent brightness
I still glow inside. It is as if the light
reflects back off the wall
and comes through my skin
into my stomach. It is as if I am having a meal
of sunlight. Around the other side

the old woman who had been carrying a chair
along with six full bags and a grandchild has died,
pre-empting what was about to be done. Now the sun

is tired and leans away behind me. The wall is lit
more quietly and projected on to it is my own shadow.
I am here, I say, *at last, I have arrived, I can be seen now*
for everything I am, ready to be examined.

Around the other side in darkness
a baby is born smiling. It is in a nest
in the trodden ground. It leaps up.

Easter tide

The first Sunday after and the choice boat went aground.
The smell of corrupt fruit soon came from its bowels,
the ladder shone blood, the ensign flew still like a trapped bird,
tattered though it was, taking up the breeze as a bird should.

The question was asked how so many fit men—if they were—
lost it so close to land, stumbling heavy through the mud,
seen by clear-eyed folk watching here, then were taken
as if they were driftwood out again. We couldn't get down.

She was beautiful. I heard mean men gasp, men who'd lost
battles with the great sea, men with tight shoulders, sniff back
gut tears when they saw her, set in the living landscape—
black rocks, a cormorant head down eyes front, the horizon.

She had no guns or enemies, she was not that kind of art,
and the burden of her cargo was hardly more than ten layers,
six thousand sheepskins perhaps, expertly stowed, a treasure.
We knew none of the men by name but by high reputation.

Into storm, eyeless away from home, she had come through,
men went out on her ends and tops as monkeys into trees.
Look now, a man in office jacket and tweed trousers stands
up to his ankles in water to be photographed next to her,

a naked child sloshes a bucket of ocean over another child
and they both scream, laughing, scampering, disaster-struck.
No-one knows how to speak of the spilt grown-up thing,
or how to reason the dead's claims on the near, elastic land.

All Souls' tide

FOR ROGER GARFITT

I have eaten the map for supper,
I have chewed and slavered its viewpoints,
bitten through the tarmac and the rock,
I have digested all the map's red lines
and all its blue, all its crosses and milestones
all its dotted lines and all its little squared
blocks—homes, farms, factories, the lot—
churned up the coniferous and non-coniferous
in my stomach, taken into my blood
the milestones and antiquities and all the names.

But the map's contours have given me guts-ache,
the field shapes have cut into my organs
making hormonal music terrifying
in its prescription: death must follow.

So I stumble out into purgatory field
hoping to get a head start on the fire,
hoping to light the straw on the fork
with my own hand, get the feel of it, get hot,
get into the swing of death,
get the murmured chorus of prayer
on my side, let the moon feast itself.

But there is no prayer here, no murmuring,
all I can do is shit map and tread mud,
no shouts make claims, no tears
give emphasis, no children tag along,
no hands cup any god's spit.
Where are the living on their feet?

God of my mistake turn your face,
dump me back into my proper place.
But no god comes either cold or hot,
either in wrath or with a small voice.
The field I have shat out is the same field
where I walked in the spring and summer,
where the sheep live wholly unaware,
where the map I have eaten will guide me.

This thirst

And myself, soaked in blood, for my song (ANEURIN, THE GODODDIN)

But still I am so thirsty. I must heave away the rocks,
I must grab away the soil,
hack away the roots, dredge the deep silt
with my shaking mouth, wrench away the squashed fossils,
release the volcanic deposits, slide away the continental plates.
And there it is!—water, boiling water, frothing, bubbling,
fuming, chaotic, delicious water!

But still I am so thirsty here on the battlefield,
I must steal water from the dead, I must catch spit
as it comes flying out of the mouths of soldiers falling,
I must suck sweat from their shirts,
I must bite out and swallow their eyes, I must drink the piss
that leaks from their bodies. Ah water!

But still I am so thirsty. I must eat grass, I must eat bushes,
hedges, I must eat whole fields of dandelions,
I must swallow the wild roses, I must gobble up the hollyhocks,
the primroses, the fruit trees, I must run my teeth
along the tree line, devouring beech, ash, oak, rowan, chestnut,
and in the inner lives of all these, in their veins—and there it is!—
in their very processes, water,
slithery, thumping, sugary, jumping water!

But still I am so thirsty. I must open my great mouth to the sky,
I must gulp the storm, devour the rainbow, I must
filter the hurricane through my nose hairs, I must devour
into my great stomach all the cloud shapes, I must swill
the drizzle, gnash at the hail stones. The spray from the sea,
the dew from the grass, the haze over all the rivers,
I must suck and suck, and there it is! water! salacious water.

But still I am so thirsty. I see you
half dancing down the hill
and I know this stirring, broken thing in me is song.
It's in your look the necessary thirst and in my eyes,
and in your limbs and in your genitals
and in your lovely playfulness. You look back at me,
you pause, you recognize, you pause, you smile,
as if nothing is out of place,
as if this, my crippling, very awkward thirst,
is bliss.

And so it was

And so it was we arrived at the Walls
        of Gloucester at Night
        and found the East Gate shut.
Tired and hungry we shouted our Lungs

sore out but got no fit Soul's Echo
        only a deranged Solo,
        some Giddypate so
mistaking our Entreaties, thinking us below

or above the earthy World, not of it,
        so we snuggled down
        horrid cold till Dawn.
By seven we were in and sat at Toast, burnt,

Ale, stale, in the House of the Mayor, Roger,
        and were offered Sheep's Brain
        in compensation
and a Blessing, the Abbot had been sent for.

Kings fall, we said, fall hard, one Edward,
        when he was in his Flesh,
        and we with News
sleeping in the Grass. We were given warmed Beds,

nice downy Beds with the Mayor's Arms on
        for floating in
        and one Forenoon
off Purgatory and an Hour more if we were gone

by Sundown, and in sleep heard the discordant
        Goblins' Song
        for having rung
the Place dry of Merriment, then went.

[Edward II was murdered at Berkeley Castle and buried
in Gloucester Cathedral in 1327]

Bach's rags

I have staggered into chapel carrying far too many books,
manuscripts most of them and most only half completed.
Waiting at the door is an indifferent messenger who makes
with his shoulders a cold show of indifference, *Carl said*
he won't be here, he's got the shakes. Sick, my first bass,
I shall be unable to test my new *Domine Deus.*

My back is raw in the draughty rehearsal room,
I am getting bog older and last night I slept
like the countess's poodle in a storm. The surface
of the new day, though, is calm
and when I have done here if the Rektor
with forced rapture does not whimsically have some bright idea
for a brand new cantata for next Sunday I shall walk
down to the river frozen over these two lovely days
and near the fine dam the beavers have made

I shall stand very still and watch the water's willing rush
in several directions at once, no involuntary push forward
exactly like the one before, each movement a rhythm
that overlays what is going before. I am a mathematician,
lights in trained voices dazzle my ears,
I am a father,
there is war across the border,
a beggar asked me beguilingly this morning for small coin,
the lowest B Flat on the organ
needs repairing. Ice under the sun
will lighten as if everything seen
can be known. I shall let good air

drain through my whole body. Folk passing
will stare hard at me, then drift away, I shall hear their tracks,
each firm, hard stud and soft sway away until I am alone again.

Please bring some socks

Please bring some socks
and if they can be smuggled in
as well the pens

and the Hebrew Bible and the dictionary
and paper. If God in his wisdom takes me
for honour's sake
that is his will but to die here

of cold in my very bones
fills me with dread. I am
like piss in a gutter
draining away
unless your graciousness
and courage save me. Smuggle in

for me the socks, my friend, Sir,
and if you will a thicker shirt
than I have here and a blanket.

[After a letter by William Tyndale in the British Library]

Father Hopkins is shy about his poems

So I went up to Father Hopkins after Mass
and I asked him, *Could I buy a book*
of your poems? He said, *Book, what book?*
I said, *Of your poems, Father.*

He looked at me
wondering, it seemed, if I was real
or whether at this early hour fasting
he had imagined me. *My book?* he asked again.
I said, *Yes, of your poems.*

He looked about him
then lowered himself on to a pew.
Do you mean there is such a book?
I said, *I assumed there was.*
He said, *Ah*, and was up and away,
murmuring to himself
some private invocation.

Private notes

IN AFFIRMATION OF MARINA TSVETAYEVA
FOR GILLIE BOLTON

Winter is all there is,
all I can hear as I walk are Spring rumours
of which poetry is the cruellest
in its promises. As if it can ease the heart,
as if it can save love, as if
it can bring you to me. I see myself pause,
I see myself turn towards the bereft willows,
I see myself I turn towards the wild dogs
at the other edge and I wonder who I am.
Am I a person? Am I praying?
What I am is out of sight,
all that can be seen is a shadowy thing.

> If all the longing in the world
> was translated into a shout
> we would all be deafened
> a thousand times over.

I am walking along a road.
The road is weakly lit
or my heart's life is so painfully lit
everything outside
seems dark in comparison.

I see the long trench there is to walk,
I hear the distance there is to be measured
in whispered exlamations: *Don't forget me!*
and, *I was here, remember!*

> Someone says, *She is in a fever,*
> but I am not, I am flying
> with one wing. *She is twisted*
> *with shame.* No,
> I am flying with one wing.

She has ideas above her station.
She has no ideas at all.
She is haunted by beauty.
She is blind. I will fly.
I will fly with my one wing.
Look, here I come now, taking off
into the clear blue.

I would have put a cushion under your head
but there was no cushion
and you were not here. There was a howling
of a prowling angel impersonating a man
and if the door had opened a flood of snow and ice
would have come in
as if it was the confused messenger. What a place to die.

Did someone come quietly
and leave a note?
Did someone come circumspectly
and leave a note?
There is no note
and I heard no-one. But surely
there has been a visit
and surely there is a note.
I have thought to myself,
Let the steps fade away
then I shall go quickly for the note.
But there is no note
and no-one has been here. But surely
there has been a visit
and surely there is a note.

The best argument
is to dress as colourfully
as dyes and materials will allow
and as the sun demands. Be bright!
I shall be bright
in my grey dress.

I prefer walking through mud
to the perfect sinewy dream of walking,
except that in the dream
I am holding your hand.

[CONTINUED

Then this happens in a room,
then that happens in a room.
We are born of soft, seeping stuff,
we are seeping stuff wrapped in skin,
we are not of our own making.
Then this happens in a room,
then that happens in a room.

Poetry will be cruel to me
all Winter in one grey
woollen dress. The fire,
my friend, has not gone out,
we can walk, it is
so beautiful here.

I don't mean he wrote poetry, his speeches *were* poetry

I don't mean he wrote poetry, his speeches *were* poetry.
When he spoke to me over coffee about the work to be done
it was poetry. So now, when I'm watering the roses
or cleaning the bath, echoes of that poetry come to me.

It is an imprecise term, *poetry*, and I am telling you only
the impression he made on me. I wonder, was he himself
aware of everything he was saying and the way he was saying it?
It was an instinctive thing for him, it came from his heart.

What I knew was a good deal less than I was sure he knew,
but partial knowledge, nonetheless, is a good start,
and I felt I was in on a pretty important unveiling of it,
it buoyed me up day by day and I did my job more capably.

He was a man, you see, who cared deeply about people,
and it made me think this was the precise essence of *soul*,
to put caring about people into those kinds of musical words
and to *do* something about it—the poetry, I can tell you,

would have been pretty hollow otherwise, I mean sterile,
I suppose I'm saying it wouldn't have been true poetry at all.
At the supermarket checkout these days and on the bus
I overhear people, and I get into conversations, always

I've been a great talker myself, and I think this is lovely,
it's real, people are saying real things, in their own, special,
individual ways about their own real lives, vividly,
but they do tend to throw it away, they throw their words

and their lives away, as if their whole being is a mere aside.
Well, he would never have done that, either for himself
or when speaking for other people. He expected good things
to happen, that was it, that was the poetry, he expected it,

and he had every intention they jolly well would happen,
he was setting about making words real there and then.

[This is a species of found poem: a reworking of a radio interview in which Barbara Castle remembered Aneurin Bevan]

6

Stretch Marks

I was plunged deep in existence, and with all that existence I prayed.
RICHARD JEFFERIES, THE STORY OF MY HEART

1. Prelude

Every nonsense has its origin in bliss,
what else to pray for
but seduction?

2. Morgan bursts in

Bathe yourself in the light! shouts Morgan, ripping away
the East wall of the hut, before I'm even out of bed.
No, thanks, I say, irritably,
I just want to get up and have a cup of tea quietly
and discreetly
and do some little jobs. Morgan sighs. *As you wish*, he says,
and puts the wall back and leaves. I can't bear the light,
its beauty hurts me,
surely he knows that. I have shells

in the crypt of the hut that need counting,
and there are skeletons of birds, too,
in boxes in the rafters, waiting to be written up,
look how plaintively they eye me—*air, air.*

3. Bronwen tells me about the piano

She was around here again
saying
There's a piano if you want it
only it's in the river.

It's in the river with the dead fish,
she says,
but it's a sunny day.

It was the sunshine made me come,
she says,
I'd been so depressed,
I'd been depressed looking out of the window

waiting for something to happen
and what happened was the sun
warmed me up so I went out into the lane
and then I saw the piano.

She is good to me.

4. Morgan pretends to be blown in

His hair is wet. He wades into the hut
kicking over the crates of beetles,
unbuttons his coat and thumps the table.

No one's theory will do for this, he says,
and I try not to flinch. None of the cats' guts
lining the walls would console him

even if they were played; if a bishop rode in
with a falcon on his arm Morgan would not
be awed. And I don't want any messages.

Now as abruptly he has gone again,
out into the rain, passion spent,
leaving me to work here as best I can
wondering what he meant.

5. Bronwen turns up during breakfast

No one will insist on a real falcon
for the entertainment, Bronwen tells me,
it will suffice for you to act one. She has turned up
during breakfast
while I am still dreaming

of a forest fire
spreading hell across the whole region,
I have been fighting the flames with a plastic cup
of rain water. *I've invited the butterflies,*

Bronwen is saying, *and the ladybirds,*
the squirrels will be here, so will the frogs
who spawn in the mouth
of the dragon, the rabbits from the old railway track

are back, the fox is coming,
so are the twins with the Bible. I love Bronwen,

I suppose, but does any of this
have my signed agreement? The heat from my dream
is overpowering, I don't know if I shall survive
at all. *You haven't*

offered me coffee, Bronwen says,
but I wasn't staying anyway,
and leaves.

6. Morgan hauls in a ragged singer who
renders a soul song

Soul is under the hammer and rain
breaks like bullets into its skin,
so sing to the tree of its deep pain

and brood upon the sludge lagoon.
Everything necessary is well known,
here we can swim and swim and drown.

Watch the maimed spider spin and spin,
here we can swim and swim and drown
and brood upon the sludge lagoon.

7. Bronwen brings blooms

She was around here again
with blooms
and I said, *At least wait till I've died,*
but she said
I've read something in the stones. Read what? I said.
I don't know, she said, *but whatever it is I thought I should*
mark the occasion. And threw the blooms at me and left.

8. Morgan drags the ragged singer back to sing
the song of the proper meeting

Enough of mere living,
let's have a real meeting,
let's pass resolutions
and make some decisions!

Mere living is lousy
but meetings are rosy,
agendas give meaning,
let's hear it for meaning!

Hooray for the issues
recorded in minutes,
if only mere living
could function like this!

9. Bronwen sends a telepathic message

She has sent me a message to say,
Put those bloody blooms in water,
so I have picked them up off the floor

and arranged them
in fresh water
in the best milk bottle I could find.

10. Morgan thinks he's a dancer

He is leaping about in the lane,
a stick in one hand,
a bunch of carrots in the other,
grinning aggressively
as if grinning has been forbidden.

11. The writing on the wall

Sometimes a story seems to begin to appear on the walls
and I think to myself
I'll get her round to tell me what it says.

The only occasion when telepathically I sent to ask her,
she took her time, came half-pissed
and when she looked at my walls no words were to be seen
and I'd forgotten the two or three I'd managed to decipher
for myself
and she didn't believe me. *Hallucinations*,
she said, and went. If a whole wall were suddenly to be covered now
and I sent for her
I don't believe she would even listen.

12. Morgan breaks my kitchen window to shout at me
what he believes is a helpful message

Someone who says she knows you
is waiting at the open gate.
I said you'd have gone to bed,
I said the lights would be out,
I said tomorrow was another day,
I said poems don't grow on trees,
I said you were busy drinking the estuary,
I said you were busy being busy,
I don't know what I said,
and she will be here by sunrise.
She will bring you a message
implying perhaps vocation.
But before she will speak to you
she will demand your life,
she will demand your larynx on its knees.

13. Bronwen comes with the bell

She comes ringing the bell
only it is rusty and doesn't ring.
She says she has dug it up in some dell
or other, *where you used to play*,

but I am in the present far away.
Listen, she says, *listen, you're not listening*,
and she shakes the bell harder and harder
till my ears bleed.

14. I lay it on the line but no one is listening

I want to know that these trees
ecstatically speechless
are in their authorized places.
Look at them: alder, rowan, willow, hawthorn,
as if by chance.

15. Bronwen wishes me Happy Birthday

'Socks were too expensive.'
    I understand.
'There was no time to write a card.'
    I understand.
'The dog ate the chocolates.'
    I understand.
'I brought you river
but it trickled through my hands.'
    'River' is an excellent name for river, I burst out,
    don't you just love the name 'river'?!
    Doesn't 'river' sound so like river?!
    I am jumping up and down now
    laughing and crying: *Oh river, oh what it is*
    to breathe the name 'river'! Is not river
    a happy thing to bring into the discussion,
    our friend river? I am thinking
    river in mountains
    where Morgan has a long, lovely walk up carrying eels.
'The grass was slippery and Morgan's in hospital.'
    And the balloons?
'Hit the barbed wire.'
    And the glo-pens?
'Went out of fashion.'

16. Morgan sends the ragged singer
    with a nicely typed question

At the post-mortem will the surgeon
find the scream, cutting through the fat,
parting the muscles and paring back the nerves,
naming the larger rivers of dry blood,
following their tracks to the places
that were so unkindly familiar, such beautiful places,
and when it's found will it be a tiny, contained scream
like vinegar about to burst
out of a pea?

17. Bronwen tells me the job

'The job is to guard the river,
what the job is
is to keep the river company
as it leaps out of the rock at the summit
and falls splashing quickly down the valley.

Keep it company, what the job is
is to help the river relax
so that it flows smoothly in spite of
rough stones and bleak turns in deep shadow,
in spite of sheep shit and buzzards' eyes,
until it joins the greater river.

Help it relax, what the job is
is to praise the river
so that it feels pleased to take the course it does,
what the job is
is not to interfere with the river doing
what it does in the way only it knows.'

18. My song to Bronwen in return

You are my field of swans,
the field is alive with swans
soaring and hitting the hedges.

It would appear that no thesis
on this subject has been formulated
or the library has been razed.

Now up and down the muddy field
the swans in their love parade
even though the sun burns them.

With no thesis I am too young.
As I paddle in the river
I can only watch and wonder.

You are my field of swans,
the field is thick with swans,
look at their clumsy big feet.

19. Morgan limps in with a message

She'll be around here again
so watch out, she's in some mood
I can tell you.
You will smell her on the wind,
you will smell her on the slightest breeze,
and she wants the flowers back, every one of them
in perfect condition,
Spring-like.

Mr Lewis, Mr Howell, Mr Lloyd and myself

1. Mr Lloyd's rags

Mr Lloyd is clothed in rags so old
no one remembers when such rags
were in fashion. Mr Howell,
who held Mr Lloyd's hand when he nearly died
wants to wash his rags but Mr Lloyd insists
on scrubbing them himself
in the river. Mr Howell, gripping Mr Lloyd's shirt,
says, *This is the shroud that wrapped the drowned god*
and carried him half dead to our shore,
at which Mr Lloyd blushes and lowers his eyes.
The shirt hangs on Mr Lloyd
like a sail, and Mr Howell blows into it
a gentle squall.

2. Mr Lewis in the hawthorn

Mr Lewis is not a goat
and I suppose he knows that, but still all afternoon
he's been on his hands and knees
with his head busy at work in the hawthorn,
bleeding. We are anxious, each of us
standing around, in our private ways,
but we must not interfere, for Mr Lewis
has his lifework to do and Mr Howell's
muttered screechings, Mr Lloyd's unspoken
urging towards caution, my humble
meandering around in case I'm wanted, all seem
beside the point. Mr Howell
is sneaking a look as if expecting treasure
to be revealed under the hedge : chocolate, for instance,
and Mr Lloyd stands alert in his damp shirt,
and as for me I write this, to heighten the record.

Is Mr Lewis really nibbling the leaves?
Mr Howell looks as if he's going to be sick,
which makes Mr Lloyd even more alert. Is Mr Lewis
becoming a stranger to us? Have we lost him now

for ever? Will we who were here
and have witnessed this moment feel one day soon
uncontrollably alone
but also blessed? Will we say, 'We knew
the old kingdom,' and wear masks
to go about our normal business?

3. Mr Howell pretends to be a red kite

Mr Howell says, *I am a stranger and can fly*,
and we give him a courteous nod
and we grin kindly, not wanting to bring him down
and we wait, dancing inwardly,
and nothing happens. We know our Mr Howell,
he's no stranger to us and he flies
only in his dreams. And yet
still we wait. Some lifting thing
is beating at our hearts
and when we look at each other
we know who we are but differently. I seem to be a mole,
Mr Lloyd is definitely a god,
Mr Lewis still has his head in the bushes,
and Mr Howell is a red kite.

So what does he want with us? I am scarcely old enough
to understand this, I am a mere blind baby
unable yet to tunnel, I am adrift
on the surface. I hear the kite strut around us
and fall over, slip and slide,
I hear it try to flap the mud off its wings
but this only makes things worse. Oh kite,
you will die of heaviness!

4. We collude

We collude in this playfulness. There are in us
secret longings, a raging gladness, a call
to stand firm in the estranged world,
to be where beauty is.

5. Mr Lewis's raft

Mr Lewis says out of the blue
I shall make a raft. The estuary, he says,
will cast him away on it into the open sea
to a far bushy island
where he will be understood. He says, casually,
I shall miss you. The raft, he explains,
will have hay in a cabin, the wind hard around it
will provide a drone, the wood through the water
will create a fugue and the wash
will be chorus. Sleep will be rhythm
and dreams will be melodies. He excites us,
me and Mr Lloyd, we feel homesick already
empathetically. *There will*, warns Mr Lloyd,
be octopus and giant squid,
the goddess of plunder will appear
in the crimson mist, but nothing
will deter Mr Lewis. All I can think to say is,
Send us a postcard. My lungs where song once was
are all bone. Mr Howell comes down
from high in the poplar
crashing into the fence. We cook supper
in silence and eat
as if we are mine shafts.

6. Like drunken gods

Our drunken gods, Mr Lloyd and Mr Howell,
are shrieking feckless jokes at each other
in the water. I wait at the gate
for when they need me to open it
so that they can re-enter in style. A nightingale
who seems to know me
comes near, sitting in the hedge, and by low tricks
I steal a feather, I pull the bird closer
and pocket an eye and while the bird sings
I capture its larynx. Now I steal a whole
gristly leg. These elements of flight I secrete
under my skin as the gate is pushed open

into my stomach by the gods returning.
With a blind lunge I grab the bird's tail, I have it.
Oh the triumph of this sublime to-do! And there's more
to accomplish: the wing feathers, every one of them,
the brain, the glands, when one day I shall reach them
over the bodies of our gods
heaped in the gateway.

7. Mr Lewis anticipates the final escapade

Mr Lewis goes down
to the beach and sits

still and alone
for twenty minutes

8. A visit from Mr & Mrs Kafka

Mr Howell waits impatiently in the poplar by the weir,
Mr Lewis is on his hands and knees beside the gate,
Mr Lloyd is painting his rags with blackberry juice
inch by inch, I am stumbling up and down the weedy lawn,
and here they come,
Mr and Mrs Kafka arm in arm glowing. Neighbours
such as this are a sight for sore eyes,
restoring our faith in the human enterprise,
and after each of us in turn does a little shy dance
Mr Howell with great style flies in with the tea and cakes
and prepares to serve
and I look into Mr Kafka's eyes: they are bright eels
at peace near the surface, catching the sun. Mrs Kafka
pours the tea, which dashes Mr Howell against rocks
until she sighs a sigh of such rapture
we all relax. Mr Kafka
squeezes her arm gently. They will have children,
two, three, six, and as sure as the grain
they will prosper. Such a harvest! Mr Howell
tries to hide Mr Lloyd's blotchy shirt with his wings
but Mr Kafka laughs such an open and infectious laugh
we all feel graced, warmed, sweeter.

9. At the edge of the sea

We bring Mr Lewis on his bed to the edge of the sea
and in turn in a line we grasp his limp hand.

Of your charity, Mr Howell hovering begins, then falters
and begins to grin and every one of us guffaws
then is silent again, except that Mr Lloyd
is crunching nuts, I myself
am dancing a silly jig, there's an impatient sigh
from Mr Howell and suddenly it has all

fallen apart, what we really wanted,
what we came for, what he is dying for.

7

Calling the rota in the upper field

Those present to do a job please listen for your name:
Job Kington—to bless the hedge.
Mick Jenkinson and Paul Holland—to dig out the stream.
Melanie Helpingale, Mary Rolands, Janine Cobbold,
Jenny Roberts-Jones and Lucy Carmine, to repair the sacred circle.
Kenneth LeGrande—to gather nettles to make soup.
Sophie Winterton—to name the spiders.
Todd Mcgorsky, Martin Singleton,
Polly Brightwell and Murray Stent—to strengthen the bridge.
Shelley Evans—to record the mushrooms.
Alison Groves—to settle the beeches.
Zoe Plimpton and Keith Wilmot—to mark out the path.
Johnson de Tombe, Millie Wellborough
and Peter Jones—to sing at the boundaries.
Philip Messinghurst and Alicia Durville—to record the smaller birds.
Lily Edwards and Catriona Bourne—to record the larger birds.
Lionel Dorking—to mend the gate.
Yasmine Rhys and Holly Baker—to plant herb seeds.
Jock Steiner and Grant West—to supply drinks.
Kate Jonkin and Roger Diamond—to supply food.
Chris Jamieson—to write a poem.

Mr Thomas, our priest

Me, I get across the bridge in three strides
and am away into the town to do business.

This morning, hearing behind me the crunch of leaves,
I looked back and saw Mr Thomas, our priest,
coming down the path to the bridge
dressed in a frock coat
and progressing on to the boards
in short steps. I thought, is this his secret wish

to hang himself out like washing over the foam
then drop and be gone
into the abyss and be borne away
by the rushing, beautiful music
to become one with the ocean? I wondered,
what would he do next? Would he

lean over the rail and retch almost?
He did.
Would he reposition himself and hold his head high?
He did.
Would he spread his arms wide and call out
in a great wail of a voice, *Heaven take me!*?
He did.

The only other witness was Mrs Lewis's pet penguin
in its caged arctic in the garden
of the Old Vicarage and it was
awestruck! So little happens
at sunrise on weekdays and this
called for a celebration, a little
flutter in the pool
and a pirouette.

At Llangynllo Station

FOR ALAN HOWARD

I reckon the ghost of Cynllo himself
materializing here on the station secretly
has corrected with a felt tip quill the spelling
of his holy name. And as no-one has reported
this malfeasance to YOUR STATION MANAGER,
smiling administratively out of his photograph
while in the flesh based thirty-eight miles away
in Hereford, England, Cynllo comes
creeping out again
from his hermit's cave in the bank of the Teme
to confront Offa who is on the 11.10
from Shrewsbury, reading *The Independent*,
while coming north on the noon train
steady from Cynghordy, fired up already,
is Owain Glyndwr, clasping his Day Saver.

So who's this Cadfael? says Cynllo,
as soon as Offa steps on to the platform, *is he one of yours?*
Offa waves him away. *Never heard of him*, he says,
Welsh name and pure melodrama, must be one of yours.
So much for your dyke, then, says Cynllo.
Hold your tongue, monk, says Offa, *I'll have you know my dyke*
has an Association.
Association, is it?! says Cynllo, nodding casually
towards the sign, I've got a railway station.

When Owain Glyndwr stands tall in the train doorway,
having pressed the blue button after it lit up,
and sees Cynllo and Offa, he knows at once what's going on.
Mae'r ffordd gen i, he says.
Speak God's language, man, says Offa.
The Way is through the heart, says Cynllo.

And the Goods pulls in
and unloads the beer
and they look again
and there's no-one there.

[CONTINUED

And the coal comes in
and is carted away
and they look again,
no deliveries today.

There seems to be peace, says Cynllo.
I don't know about that, says Owain, *now I'm back, there's work to do.*
You've got your Prince, says Offa, and twenty-five years a Prince.
But no woman priests, says Cynllo, with a certain ambivalence.
Women priests!? says Glyndwr, *let them wash socks!*

The 17.23 can be heard down the valley,
the 16.14 is on its way from Shrewsbury.

When shall we three meet again?

When the llan yields up its kin
at the resurrection.

When the dyke is fierce with song
in the fullness of the moon.

When the ffordd through wind and rain
leads to parliament again.

And what about the World Cup? says Cynllo.
You mean someone's found the Grail? says Offa.
Dean Saunders should be there, says Glyndwr.

Travel poem

I took a little Holub on the train
from Birmingham New Street to Great Malvern
via Prague
where on the steps of the cathedral
someone in a wheelchair smiling
as if I was an old friend
gave me a loaf of dark bread
and when hungrily I bit deep into it
I got a beetle in my mouth
who called out to me cheerfully,
It's OK, this is poetry.

I spat the beetle out on to my hand
and from deep in my heart said 'Thank you'.
Now dissect me, it said, *dissect, dissect,*
and fell back unconscious,
flat and splayed out on a tomb.

Look at the train driver now
red in the face, waving all his arms
and shouting frantically,
We're leaving, brother,
and me shouting back,
I must do this trick.

I pared back the beetle's diaphragm
and I heard singing. It was of course angels,
but my train was waiting.

I was asleep when we arrived at Great Malvern.
The Senior Conductor woke me and urged me off:
Detours like that, Sir, if you'll beg my pardon,
require Head Office's written permission.

[The 'little Holub' is the Czech poet Miroslav Holub's *Selected Poems*, in the Penguin Modern European Poets series, 1967]

A woman was round here selling blankets

A woman was round here selling blankets
and although I didn't need a blanket
I bought one, a large blue one, *like the sea*,
I said, but she feigned barrenness.
Seeing her blue eyes flicker, I said,
I wonder how many blue blankets end to end
would make a replica
of the River Avon, but she was holding out her hand
for the money
and not listening to me. Giving her a note I said,
Blankets are needed urgently in war,
and as she was giving me my change, *Have you thought*
of finding some bloody war
to sell these in? But she was repacking her bag
and her hair was falling over her eyes
and I was holding my blanket tight and she was up
as far as her bent back would go
and away to the next house. I called after her
with what I imagined was a plaintive sound,
Blue is sky as well and wisteria
and lazuli
and cold.

8

Poem

FOR ROY FISHER
IN THE YEAR OF HIS 65TH BIRTHDAY

knees up

o

Brum bard

above the drone

A man called James Dye

Nobody ever gets beaten up in my poems
or cuts their own wrists
or dies in a car crash. Take James Dye, for instance,
his bursts of translucent energy
are very quiet. Saying nothing to anyone
he went by bus last week into town, sallied up New Street,
said 'Good morning' to the *Iron Man*,
'Hi' to the Floozie and 'Your majesty' to *Victoria*,
paused and shrugged where *Diana* had stood and where her name is,
bought an old *Villa* shirt in the *Rag Market*, then a carrot
from Carl in the fruit and veg market by *St Martin's* and ate it,
hung around the *Pavilions*, overhearing snatches of conversation,
enjoying perfume up and down in the lift,
having his spine tingled by smiles between lovers,
then silently on New Street Station
applauded the *Devon Scot*, the *Pines Express*,
the *Armada*
and *Laurence Olivier*, then went home
and watched *Midlands Today*.

James Dye, curled up with crisps of an evening
and a hot chocolate,
watches *Casualty*, too, of course, and *Taggart*,
The Bill and *The X-Files*—plenty of beatings-up
betrayals, confrontations, blood and hurt.
My poems know this mayhem is there all right
but prefer to follow people like James
on his days out.

Nine tables

CANNON HILL PARK, BIRMINGHAM. FOR LENNY ALSOP

Four dozen geese parade up and down the grass,
one moorhen on the lake minds its own business,
two ducks fight in a circle that is endless,
the four arms of the windmill are locked in silence,
two poplar trees are half way to the heavens,

and nobody is sitting at nine tables.

The park spins around one large imported stone.
In one corner of the park is the dome frame
my children scare me by climbing up to slide down.
South of that is the wood where the frogs come.
From the East corner we catch the 35 bus home.
In the North by the Arts Centre I am writing this poem,

and nobody is sitting at nine tables.

No-one lives on the island at DANGER DEEP WATER.
The bell of the *Birmingham* sings out no watches.
No-one sees light through the windows of the saloon bar
of the Golden Lion. Car after car and lorries and buses
beating the bounds of the park burn the air
in this district of everywhere with dull grey anger,

and nobody is sitting at nine tables.

We have no abiding city, all flesh is as grass.
People come and go rehearsing their childhoods.
Bless me mud after rain for I have fallen into dryness.
Look how my praising hands are trapped at my sides,
how my feet leave surface marks to no purpose,

and nobody is sitting at nine tables.

Two other fellas

FOR DAVE REEVES

At the bus stop in Digbeth one man says to another man,
Wasn't it you I saw last year in the Kings Head in Bilston?
No, the second man says, *I've never been north of Quinton*,
to which the first man replies,
Neither have I, it must have been two other fellas.

When the bus comes they wave it away.

Wasn't it you I pulled out of the Birmingham and Worcester canal?
Not me, but thank you, anyway.
I wasn't there either, it must have been two other fellas.

When the next bus comes they wave it away.

Weren't you the bastard that ran off with my wife to Lichfield?
Not me, friend.
No, well it must have been two other fellas.

When the next bus comes they wave it away.

You were the man who saved the penalty I took in that Villa final.
Me with my limp?
Nor me with my back. Must have been two other fellas.

Now they want to get on the bus
but no bus comes and they wait in silence

until one of them, pacing up and down, says

You sent me into the world to redeem the world.
Ay, the second man says, *that was us, that was us.*

[I am indebted to Billy Teare, from whom I heard the basic anecdote
that started me off on the poem, at the storytelling Festival of the Edge]

Looking for God in the waters

ON A MAVERICKS BOAT TRIP ON THE BIRMINGHAM CANALS, SEPTEMBER 1997. FOR TESSA LOWE

The sunlight is reflected,
so are the nettles,
the willows and the sycamores.
If all our eyes leaned over the edge of the boat
we, too, would be reflected and some of us
no doubt would fall in, enamoured
of the illusion of dark deep. There are blue patches
on the surface where the sky is reflected
and reddish-brown of brick wall,
then someone from behind a wall throws a stone
and shatters a window. And we thought this
was an oasis. Where, I wonder, is God
with his ukulele? A sofa is reflected now
in a deserted shack with no front to it
where no-one sits watching
or playing music as the boat passes. God
was here perhaps
in the olde days. Inside the boat
there are ceiling lights: pink, blue, orange, green,
a sparse little overhead flower garden.
We pass factory windows broken long since,
alsatians in a boat yard making enemies of us,
buddleia growing out of walls which
if we are butterflies
will be our friend.

Me and Myfanwy in town

Myfanwy, too, had come for the counselling
but Mrs Rees-Jones had been taken ill at short notice.
We sat there not knowing what to do with ourselves.
We got chatting and went for a cappuccino.

Dark shadows had been cast over both our lives.
What I need, I said, *is to live with paradox.*
What I need, Myfanwy said, *is a good fuck. Mrs R-J*
was going to give me permission, she promised.

We went to the Nature Centre and in the aquarium
watched some huge, exotic goldfish
suck the thick glass. Outside, the sky had turned grey
and I offered Myfanwy in her thin blouse my jacket.
She declined abruptly. This hurt me.

We strolled to the bus stop and waited. Myfanwy leaned back
hard against the post and I hopped up and down
pretending I needed to keep warm,
until the No. 63 came. We got off at the university
where Myfanwy hung around outside the shop
while I bought a Turkish Delight to share. I said,
concerned to get it right and choosing my moment,
Do you value the lyric impulse? and she said she did, she did,
she valued it greatly, looking straight at me.

We went into town on a 21, it was Late Night Shopping.
We went into Waterstone's and Marks & Spencer's
and deep into GAP, looking, almost touching. I said,
Shall we go to the art gallery? Myfanwy—oh Myfanwy—
looked into my eyes, stroked my arm
and said, honestly, she'd rather sit by the fountain,
so we sat dangling our feet almost into the water.

I picked up a leaf in Victoria Square to keep with me
because this day would hold a special memory,
then Myfanwy needed to go to a loo
and I knew where one was and, after she emerged again
into the Spring twilight, I said, *Days are what we live in*,
and she said, *Yes*, nodding, and looked at me oddly,
while again touching me, my cheek this time,
with her little finger, and then went away,
back to her room, she joked, to kill herself.

Praise poem

1.
Brian Butler was on our roof again this week
looking for wherever it was the water
was coming through and dripping
on to the stairs. He found it where the roofs joined
and put new zinc in, then patched up some other corners.
I trust him to tell me what really
needs doing and to do it well.

I said, *The fence is still standing.*
Oh, he said, *did I do that?*
You did, I said, *you put in new supports.*
What's your son doing, he said, *your eldest?*—
drinking the tea I gave him, standing at the back door
with a cigarette in his other hand.
He's just joined Dawn Printers, I said.
Mine got his degree in geology, he said, *and is out in Africa.*
I said, *How's business?*
Not so good, he said, *people aren't spending money.*
He'll be back again any time we need a job doing
and I'm blessed he's there
on the end of the phone.

2.
When they were something like four and three years old
I made a climbing frame for Cressy and Caleb—
Josh and Gabriel helped me. The man at York Supplies
—all these years and I don't know his name
though he welcomes me always with mine—
had helped me decide the wood,
had cut it for me, advised me on the structure
and delivered the uprights and planks to our house.

When several days later the structure was in place
here in the back garden
he came round and I asked what he thought,
at which without a word
he leapt to the top and jumped up and down on it.
Praise to him for this act of faith.

[CONTINUED

3.
Philip Atkinson is the son at Atkinson and Son.
I remember his father still around the garage
but not with his head seriously in engines.
Philip Atkinson is my car's doctor, the consultation
is never rushed and the manner
would do any surgery proud. Once I was sitting around
with a group of clergy and health workers
talking about what mattered to us and I said
it mattered to me that near where I live there's a skilled
and trustworthy car mechanic. They looked at me
a bit oddly. Last year I drove back from Wales
having gently hit a car park gate at Laky Vyrnwy
and another time one of the dashboard dials

started flickering over to danger, and every September
there's the M.O.T.. *Leave it with me,* he says, *say three
this afternoon?* When I go back it's done
and he'll post the bill, he says, through my letter box.
He's always said this and has never done it. Each time
I go back and pay
glad of the friendly continuity.

4.
At Tanners Green there's a five barred gate
and on it a notice that says simply, BUNGALOW.
You go down the lane through the bushes
and there's his shack of a house like something
that seems to have been transported
from a frontier. But this is
a kind of frontier. John Williams is here alone
except for how many free range hens? Dozens?
Hundreds? I wonder what his secret is,
always rosy cheeked and smiling,
always welcoming. Some time ago he'd seen my name
in the newspaper and he told me he was at school
with Geoffrey Hill: *We played cricket together.*

I take my dozen large and as I approach the road
all my busyness and anxiety and hurt is collected
back into myself, as if I'd left it at the gate. But I glow too

a little more than I did. All these many years now
and still when I care to drive out there
he comes to the open verandah—What a routine
he must have: egg boxes, hens, eggs, egg boxes,
and daily the music of hens—and I wonder again
what his secret is.

[The man at York Supplies is John Jaffa]

9

On what island?

On what island shall we hold the party?
On a dead fish floating in the river?
On a ball bouncing along the motorway?
On a planet rolling in space?

On what island shall we hold the party?
On a sceptred isle with spoils privately?
On a video replaying the World Cup for ever?
On a Bosnian child's head?

On what island shall we hold the party?
On a poem balancing on the page?
On Atlantis?
On purpose?

And did those feet

A POEM FOR THE MILLENNIUM

And did those feet in ancient time—
He splutters, spitting blood,
walk upon—
and he walks a little,
then opens his mouth again, this time
trying to sing, in a low hoarse voice,
And did those feet in ancient time
walk upon England's—
and he spits more blood,

and he walks a few steps more,
then starts to mouth again, trying hard
to sing it loud, clear,
spitting phlegm and blood:
And did those feet in ancient time—
and he walks a few steps more—
walk upon England's mountains—
then begins again: *And did those feet—*
and limps a few more steps
choking on blood. Thirsting
he closes his eyes,
he has the word *home*,
he knows the word *home*,
he tries to remember what *home* was,

and he falls,
and gets up
and walks a few more steps
through the red grass, and shapes his hands
trying to make them sing,
and now mouthing the words,
And did those feet in ancient time
walk upon England's mountains green
and did the countenance divine—
and falls again,
and no rains come,
no pleasant storm, no thunder,
no brilliance. *And did those feet*
walk upon—he walks
and falls again, singing, singing.

Sarajevo Sonata

Never send to know for whom the bell tolls,
it tolls for thee.
JOHN DONNE

Shell the schoolhouse!
Shell the yard!
Cook the kids till break time,
choke their every word!

Keep me—

Shell the classrooms!
Shell the lot!
Kiddie meat will make us rich,
kiddie meat,
kiddie meat.

Keep me—

We can sell their bones to make bombs,
their livers for conference buffets,
their eyes can go into the Internet.

Keep me as the apple of an eye.

We can sell their genitals for missile oil.

That kid's mine!
No, that one's mine!

Hide me—

That one's mine!
No, that corpse is mine!

Hide me—

That body's mine!
No, that one's mine!

Hide me under the shadow of thy wings.

The ornamental teapots
are precisely in their place
on the polished mantlepiece.

[CONTINUED

I was only hitchhiking
but found myself in Tito's procession,
children lined the route
waving their eggs and sperm.

The ornamental teapots
precisely—

My brother liked to play at fighting.

The pigeons are scattering.

My brother liked to play at fighting
until the real thing
came to his safe haven
and killed him. 'When the shelling stops,'
he had said, 'I shall go for
        water
        and potatoes,
        flour
        and olives,
        paper.'

The ornamental teapots
precisely in their place
on the polished mantlepiece
were no defence.

Make peace, you bastards!
—but the words bounce off
all the walls of the world
and come back: make peace,
                you bastard!

My brother liked to play—

The ornamental teapots did their
silent and static conga
representing us
at the heart of the universe.

We scraped him off the market place
and sent him home to Mum,—

The pigeons are scattering,
leaving their feathers behind.

We gathered up his fingernails
and posted them to Dad,
it was the prettiest parcel post
he had ever had.

The pigeons are scattering,
leaving their bones behind.

Glory, glory, hallelujah!—

The River Miljacka is a tributary
of the River Wye and vice versa,
ask the fish
who they'd prefer
to be killed and eaten by.

We couldn't find his rib-cage
so we left it in the rain,
some bits of him were far too small,
we flushed them down the drain.

Glory, glory—

The pigeons are scattering,
leaving their bodies behind.

My brother liked to play at fighting.

Glory, glory, hallelujah,
teacher hit me with the ruler!
Glory, glory,

[This poem was written to the set theme at the Hay-on-Wye Poetry Squantum in 1995. The lines in italics are to be sung; the first are a versicle and response from the Office of Compline; the final sections come from the Battle Hymn of the Republic via Boy Scout versions of decades ago]

The common

So we strode off, the three of us, to break down the fences.
We sang the round of the widows of the fertile valley.
Neighbours watched us, knowing what we were about to do.
When we arrived men set dogs on us and threw bricks.

Some people watching spat and swore, taking against us,
standing by while the bricks flew and the dogs leapt.
The fences stood tight between us and the sweet new life
everyone present knew was our prize if could win it.

Meg said, *Speak a prayer*, and I said, *No*. Alli too said, *No*,
then prayed: *Spirits of water, air, love, the deep well at Gwerin,*
Susan and Jane's pottery, chianti, our comfy old armchair,
the craft collective, clematis, till a fierce flying brick hit Meg hard

and she fell. Eyes of my soul. Some standing by hooted
and cheered and when Alli was felled by a dog some friends
as we'd thought jeered and punched the air. I rushed on
blindly into the barbed wire and fell yelling back.

People dispersed then, calling as they went, *Stupid farts,*
shit-bags, and some cheered in mock salute, others
exchanged winks with the men as they called their dogs off,
a few shouted, *Good try!, See you in the pub! Fucking great!*

Then we were alone in a sublime silence. Blood dripped
into high, lovely grasses, a mouse rushed by and no buzzard
came after it, a cow eyed us from across the river, a woodpecker
knock-knocked our quick breathing, ants were on Alli's leg.

Was this for singing? Was our bleeding failure there a fit tune?
River washed us, we bandaged each other with socks,
with shirt sleeves, arms, eyes. Meg cried, shouting, *Shit! Shit!*
Alli began to make new, bold plans. I have written this.

High summer in the middle world

The doors have slid open
on to the wrong room.
The middle world I lived in yesterday
has gone. It's an ante-room of hell
I'm in. It's the engine room

of the battleship the boy I was
was in. I can still smell
that metal, I panic

to get out on deck again. Some kind of fit
home has
has been displaced. Hell, then,

is where I can't breathe, where I am all right
but imprisoned
in too hot a light.

As the sheep gather under the tree
so my thoughts gather in me,
refugees from God's hot breath:
this far, no further,
or be cooked in thought. *The sweat tent*

is open, ladies and gentlemen,
says God, *now bathe in thought.*
The rhododendron

seems to love it, and the dandelion,
the foxgloves and the lupin,

pure thought, pure holding open.

Parents shout at children,
children shout at parents,
parents are bigger. The driver
shouts at another driver
and the other driver shouts back,

this mundane anger
wallpapers the middle world
and flakes off.
We are skinning ourselves alive.

When better to read about extreme unkindness?

When better to read about the extreme unkindness
done to people by people
than in those precious minutes before sleep?
When better to be so hurt? When better
to shiver and squirm than in the cuddly comfort
of my own bed? And to take into dream
those hurts impossible to reconcile
during daylight. Children caught weeing
against the wall of the barracks
when forbidden to wee anywhere at all all night long
had small sticks threaded into their penises
which were then hit to break the sticks inside,
after which they whimpered and wee'd only blood.
Babies were thrown in through the door
in the extreme cold
who during the night ate their own fingers
down to the bone and then died—
take these into dream. And every day in the street
I see children hurt. Take into dream the parental taunts
and the secret beatings, take the utter fear into dream,
take the faces turned away, the silence
in response to simple needs, take the confused tears,
take the ache into adulthood. Take the thread of survival
into that other place.

[The book was Binjamin Wilkomirski's *Fragments*, translated from the German by Carol Brown Janeway]

This is who we are

FOR THE PEOPLE GATHERED AT BISHOPSWOOD

And we were made for this
my friends
we were made for this,
this is who we are,
this is who we are.

Nothing can be said
and something must be said.

There is nothing to say
and everything to say.

Who knows who we are
or what we are?
But still we are,
but still we are.

This is us in a warm room somewhere
and no echoes back
from anywhere out there,
this is who we are,
this is who we are.

This is us in a corner of the universe
who love
and are loved,
this is us,
this is us.

We were made for this
my friends
we were made for this,

this is who we are,
this is who we are.

[After the minibus crash on the M40 in November 1993, some of the families and friends of the Hagley School pupils and their teacher who were killed, met monthly at the Bishopswood Environmental Centre in Worcestershire. I was an invited outsider.]

As you speak I look at your neck

IN CELEBRATION OF KEN SARO-WIWA, SPEAKING ON TELEVISION
AFTER HE WAS HANGED TO DEATH, NOVEMBER 1995
FOR STEWART BROWN

You speak about gas flare
after gas flare after gas flare
polluting your people's air,
and as you speak
I look at your neck.

You speak about big, big money
from the oil under your people's land
and your people still in poverty,
and as you speak
I look at your neck.

Our land has a heavy rainfall,
the rain has been turned acid,
now the soil is infertile,
we can no longer supply bread,
and as you speak
I look at your neck.

You indict Shell,
you say Shell has made a hell
of Ogoni land. You anticipate
imprisonment
as if it is a literary prize,
and as you speak
I look at your neck.

You say your art must be combative,
change the way people live,
give them inner vigour
to defy outer fracture,
and as you speak
I look at your neck.

You speak not of selling your books
but of getting power off people's backs,
the stories I tell in my books
are a necessary politics,
and as you speak
I look at your neck.

I swear by the music

I swear by the music of the expanding universe
and by the eloquence of the good in all of us
that I will excite the sick and the well
by the severity of my kindness
to a wholeness of purpose. I shall apply my knowledge,
curiosity, ignorance and ability to listen.

I shall co-operate with wondering practitioners
in the arts and the sciences,
with all who care for people's bodies and souls,
so that the whole person in relationship
shall be kept in view, their aspirations and their unease.

The secrets of the universal mind
I shall try to unravel to yield beauty and truth.
The fearful and sublime secrets told to me in confidence
I shall keep safe in my own heart.

I will not knowingly do harm to those in my care,
I will smile at them
and encourage them to attend to their dreams
and so hear the voices of their inner strangers.

If I keep to this oath I shall hope for the respect of my teachers,
and of those in my care and of the community,
and to be healed even as I am able to heal.

[This is a revised version of my rewriting of the Hippocratic Oath,
commissioned originally by *The Observer* and published in July 1997]

The prisoner reads his poem

FOR NIGEL MOFFATT, WRITER IN RESIDENCE,
SHREWSBURY PRISON, NOVEMBER 1997

I am sitting behind, in line,
the Mayor, the Governor, the Director General and the MP.
An inmate comes to the microphone
and reads his poem. There has been talk in the speeches
about the value of self-expression and of the self-respect
prisoners may regain through writing. It is a good thing,
the Home Secretary has said in a message,
that such programmes of work are undertaken,
and is sorry not to be able to attend in person.
I am sitting
in the prison hall at the book launch, behind, in line,
the Mayor, the Governor, the Director General and the MP,
as an inmate comes to the microphone
and reads his poem.

Poetry is good for him, they have said,
the Mayor, the Governor, the Director General and the MP,
and now they have sat and listened to his poem.

The Mayor, the Governor, the Director General and the MP
go back to their systems,
I go back home on the train,
and Hansel Shepherd goes back to his cell,
his poem, I suppose,
still clamouring inside him.

We are all inmates of the world,
our mouths open and close, open and close.

[Hansel Shepherd's poem is in the anthology, *Inside*,
published by HM Prison Shrewsbury]

In the Endoscopy Suite

My penis is held poking through a hole in a blue sheet.
The doctor has packed something wet around it. He says,
I shall inject some anaesthetic, which will sting. It stings.
My coat and trousers are in a black bag on a chair
and I am lying on my back, stretched out.

The tube slides in. *This*, he says, matter-of-factly,
will hurt for a moment as it goes through the sphincter.
It hurts and a good strong *Bloody hell!* tides me over.
Sorry, he says, and a friendly black nurse standing by me
like a mother, seems to be holding me. She has a warm
chuckling laugh and I feel she feels my pain.

The man looks into my bladder through the telescope.
He says, *I see no growths or stones.*
His eye hard on, he says, *What do you know about the prostate?*
I reply, conversationally, *I understand it can become infected
and enlarged, inflammation is common,
the normal blood supply is not good.*

A student doctor by the doctor's side
looks down a tributary tube.
Whatever she sees or thinks, her voice, her eyes,
the whole apprenticeship of her face stays silent.

I'd like to be in an aeroplane again,
bouncing, swimming in air, whimsying my eyes down
between the tidal clouds at the tiddly ships
crossing the white-blue, folding waves. *Your prostate*, he says,
*is its normal size. But inflamed. There is no sign of cancer,
drink extra today, water and so on, drain the system out.*
In my bladder tides will continue to roll
until the moon says *Enough*.

On the bus, with my trousers and coat back on,
as the anaesthetic fades I feel newly named.
My penis, keeping itself to itself,
is sore. My whole body feels shocked
as if having responded to a strange calling.

Playing the stories

FOR MALCOLM RIGLER

Say what you have to say, poem!
You've been invited here,
what do you know?

I see people waving to each other
if they have a spare moment
waving to each other
from one parallel treadmill elegantly
to another. I see people
contemplating their career moves,
publishing their latest research findings.
In their separate buildings they are
building upon *fundamental* principles,
ascending their *ladders* of progress
piling up their *building blocks* of ideas.
We are running up and down inside our building
while they are running up and down inside theirs
and them over there are running up and down inside theirs.
We are *filing* our findings
and *stacking* our knowledge
while they *stack* theirs
and them over there *stack* theirs.

Enough of that, poem!
Say something else,
something happy.

Happy co-incidence is a dance,
serendipity is its rule,
letting go is its power,
relativity is its music,
interaction is its joy,
fluidity is its ethic
in perpetuum mobile.
My change affects your change,
yours affects mine, the world every moment
is what it is through the interaction of all the changes

and there is no neutral viewing platform, no vantage point
of not-change. Passivity, my friends,
is also relationship.

Yes, but enough of that, poem!
Let's have some real stories.
Let's play at stories.

Here we are in a room together
naked. We are in the mortuary,
this is an after-death experience.

Not that story.

We are in our blouses, t-shirts, skirts or shorts
—it's an anarchy of colour—
on the beach, running in and out of the sea,
eating our ice creams, playing a test match
on sand where the ball never bounces,

and now, ageing as we are,
we have escaped in here to get away from the burning sun
but we still want fun: shall we
play poker?
look into each other's cameras?
swap anecdotes about previous holidays?

Not that story.

What we are, truly, in this room
is a company of character actors.
The lion tamer is here, and the bishop,
the football manager and the groundsman,
the Lady of the Manor, the traveller full of tall stories,
the detective, the seed merchant, the opera singer,
the merchant ship's captain, the actor acting the actor,
the window cleaner, the sprightly politician,
the corner shopkeeper . . .

But what does any of this mean now,
for the truth is we are refugees. We have straggled in here
with nowhere to go on to
and nowhere to go back to
and this evening after being given a mug of tea
and a bowl of soup

[CONTINUED

we will be listed. Do you know
we had lives once? We were somebody. People knew
who we were,
greeted us in the street, waved as we passed in our cars, and now
do we have names even? We will be given new names
for convenience,
names that happen easily to trip off the tongue
of the officials who will list us.

Not that story.

What we are, really,
is a group of patients, thrown together in the television room,
sitting around
in our starched dressing gowns,
waiting for news of tests,
waiting in this nameless sanctuary
for relatives or friends to come in and see us,
and we are afraid. Speak to us, somebody,
inarticulately but honestly,

with faith in the moment itself
now that the painkillers
are at the end of their effectiveness
and the day is dull and shadowy
and time has come back and is weighing heavy,
and there will have been love.

Not that story.

So, truly, we are here for a wedding. Health is to be married to Arts
and we're all dressed up in our brightest white,
we're all bridesmaids with the giggles—

And we want to play!

For who are we, really? We are children, of course,
we are a room full of restless kids. We hear
confusion, we know the unspoken
discomforts, we see people turn away,
we are led on, we ask silly questions,
we have not been long in this world
where birds sing in trees
and grain grows silently

and waves hit the sand, retreat,
come again, retreat again,
and grass grows through the city pavements.
We hear laughter
and we laugh, we know rude jokes,
we get shouted at, we want to play,
we want to test ourselves, we want to make a world.
We get patted on the head. So in our imaginations
we play
beautifully, secretly.

[Dr Malcolm Rigler at Withymoor Surgery, in Dudley in the West Midlands, commissioned this poem for the visit of the Chief Medical Officer, Sir Kenneth Calman, in January 1997, when he met senior health and education officers and others to discuss 'arts and health' in the Borough. The poem was read on that occasion in Thorns School.]

Biographical note

David Hart was born in 1940 in Aberystwyth, Wales, and for the past more than twenty-five years has lived in Birmingham. He has been, amongst other things, an Anglican university chaplain, a playwright and a theatre critic, and for nearly fifteen years up until 1997 was at first Drama and Literature then Literature Officer part-time for West Midlands Arts. He started the Hay-on-Wye Festival Poetry Squantum and edited the book of the first, *Border Country* (1991), and published *Poetry Listing,* a review listing of new poetry, for five issues to 1993. He has contributed to the growing movement linking arts and health and has compiled and edited a book of interviews with General Practitioners, with related essays, *What are doctors for?* (1997). He won the BBC R4 *Afternoon Shift*'s nonsense poem competition 1997 and was a prizewinner in the Waterstone's art criticism competition 1997. He won the 1997 Common Ground / Blue Nose Poetry Field Days competition and is the 1997-98 Birmingham Poet Laureate.

Setting the Poem to Words brings together new poems with poems published in magazines and anthologies, including prize-winning poems. These include first prize in the National Poetry Competition 1994 and a runner-up prize in the same competition in 1996, the Irish National Poetry Competition prize 1996 and first in the Lincolnshire Festival Competition 1995, as well as prizes in the *Sheffield Thursday*, Exeter, Bridport, Toc H and other competitions.